Books by Dr. Bill Miller

Ministry:

Narrow is the Gate: An Introduction to the Christian Religion
Spirit Led Christian
The Power of a Grateful Heart
Prosperity School...Straight from the Bible
Life Changing Financial Principles...Straight from the Bible
The New Testament Tithe...A Biblical Way to Honor God

Practical Financial Teaching Books:

Employee to Employer in 90 Days
Start a Home Business in 30 Days
Credit Repair That Reduces Monthly Payments
Budget Yourself to Financial Victory
Debt SmashDown: Payment Strategies that Succeed

History:

An Inauspicious Hero...The Story of Sumner Bacon
The Influence of Christianity on Early Texas History

Church Administration (out of print):

Policy Administration in the Local Church
A Generic Policy Manual for the Local Church
Deacon Operating and Policy Manual
Policy Manual for the Children's Ministry
New Members Teaching Guide for the Local Church

BORDER TRUTH

Straight from the Bible

Dr. Bill Miller

Border Truth

Granbury, Texas
Original publication August 2018 as *The Truth About Open Borders*
Rewritten and published under a separate ISBN Spring of 2021

Illustrations by *Cody Stromberg Artworks*, Granbury, Texas
Cover Design by *Monoliver Marketing*, Glen Rose, Texas
Cover Editing by *Maverick Book Services*, Cebu City, PHL

Make A Way Ministries
Granbury, Texas

ISBN: 978-0-9700803-2-5

WHAT CHRISTIAN LEADERS ARE SAYING ABOUT THIS BOOK

>Pastor Jerry Masden, CEO of Christian Values Summit

"Bill Miller has done his homework to show from Scripture that God is NOT pro open borders and that actually He has a special purpose for them. This book gives clarity to a really important subject of the day...Pastors in particular should read it and consider some adjustments to their world view...as appropriate."

>U.S. Pastor Council

More than 1,500 pastors in 22 states have signed the Pastors' Declaration on Border Security and Immigration Reform which challenges our elected officials to lay aside partisan politics and develop real solutions to the escalating illegal immigration crisis and the security of our national borders. (See Appendix B in this book)

>Ron Sutton, President, Hood County Conservatives

"Having secure borders is a fundamental Conservative objective which is only made stronger by connecting it to Scripture. Author Bill Miller has more than adequately accomplished that connection in this special book."

Contents

Introduction

The way I see things: it's not just the U.S. that's divided these days, it's the whole world. Some see it as *politically* divided, which of course we are. But politics isn't the real crux of it because many things that divide us in America are the same issues that divide people all over the world. We don't all have the same politics but we *do* have common issues we're divided about.

It also seems that most people including a lot of Church folks are trying their best to keep the focus on politics instead of facing the real issue. But they ALL know in their hearts it's something else, something way more than politics and it's something they want to avoid dealing with.

The truth is, we're all involved in an ever-widening *spiritual* division and it's all about the Christian Bible, aka the *Word of God*. To some of us it seems like God is making an announcement: *It's time for you to choose. I have set before you life and death, the blessing or the curse.*[1] *So choose NOW because I'm about ready to get on with the rest of eternity!*

In sum, the division we're facing involves a confrontation between what the world calls *Political Correctness* and *Biblical Correctness*. The good news is, of course, that the Bible eventually wins and that will be the end of the confrontation. But in the meantime, there is a list of counterfeit values that constitute *Political Correctness* and each of them opposes a true and righteous value from the Word of God. In the near term, the response of true Christians must be to stand for biblical values even as the world is drawn to the more popular set of PC values.

One of the most prominent set of counterfeit values involves the subject of how to deal with undocumented aliens together with its related subtopics of immigration, naturalization, amnesty, DACA, the elimination of ICE, sanctuary cities, refugees, *coyotes,* the Border Wall and all the rest of the issues covered by this particular political category. None of these subtopics is particularly new, but what's presented in this book is that they are pitted against the Christian Bible. What does the Bible actually say about the borders of nations and their interaction with "visitors" from other countries? How do the pursuits of Christian love and charity fit into a Christian world view of nations and their borders?

This book has been written for people who want to know the truth about a subject that traditionally hasn't received much attention in the Church. Indeed, Christians have tended to endorse political rhetoric or the World's "feel-good" edicts instead of looking to the Word of God. My intent is that readers come to a more informed understanding of how God is looking at our *borders* so that we can agree with Him and pass the truth on to others.

Dr. Bill Miller (June 2021)

KEY SCRIPTURES

"The God who made the world and all things in it...gives to all people life and breath and all things; and He made from one man every nation of mankind to live on all the face of the earth, having determined their appointed times and the BOUNDARIES of their habitation, that they would seek God..."

Acts 17: 24-26
New American Standard

"...I am the way, and the truth, and the life; no one comes to the Father but through Me."

John 14:6
New American Standard

BORDER TRUTH

Straight from the Bible

"I have given them your Word and the world has hated them because they are not of the world, even as I am not of the world."

John 17:14
New American Standard

One:

A Monumental Confrontation

One of the great polarizing issues of our day concerns the administration of our borders. On the one hand, borders define nations and the geographic limits of each government's responsibility and protection. They also provide a basis for the development of particular cultures. Indeed, we have always had borders but in today's environment, a growing number of people have become determined to do away with America's borders so that they can move about freely wherever and whenever they want to. Certainly, there are two distinct bodies of opinion about this subject but why has it in just the last few years become so politically oriented and such a heated wellspring of division?

These are very momentous times we're living through, probably the most important in the history of the world, except of course for those special 33-years when the Word became flesh and came to earth to dwell among His people.[2] I use the word *momentous* because the planet has become just about fully divided over what seems at first to be a group of political issues but what we're actually experiencing is a monumental confrontation over the Christian Bible. And, as we're about to see, our border situation is one of the major parts of that confrontation which makes it, perhaps surprisingly, a bible-based issue.

Jesus confirmed that the Word He gave us is TRUTH. He also said that it separates us from the World and causes it to hate us.[3] In sum, the Word of God has *itself* divided the people of the world into two camps: there are those who accept it in their minds and hearts as absolute truth and there's everybody else. The *"everybody else"* group rejects all or part of the Word and it is much larger than the truth group. Moreover, since the Word is absolute truth, there are only these two possible groups that we can all be a part of: we either accept the totality of the Word as absolute truth or reject it either partially or totally.

The main reason people reject the truth so strenuously is because it shines light on our sin.[4] That is one of the things the Word does simply by its nature. It reveals our sin and provides irrefutable confirmation that we need some kind of special power to help us be reconciled to the one true God. When I was a sinner, I rejected His offer of reconciliation so I could continue with my life the way I wanted it to be, sin and all. My mind was blinded to the ways of God[5] and I didn't want to hear the truth. I knew there was a God but I didn't want to focus on it too long, and I sure didn't want to stop sinning.

Fortunately, I eventually saw the Light and changed my attitude. But most people on the planet are refusing to undergo the necessary change. As time has gone on with the ever-declining influence of God in the American culture, the *"everybody-else"* group has of late scurried to invent their own code of morality in order to finally replace the Bible they are so committed to rejecting. For the sake of simplicity, I will call that code *Political Correctness* and refer to it hereafter as *PC*.

PC is comprised of an ever-changing list of values and mores including ways of speaking and believing that serve to *"authenticate"* one's personal morality. You are either a good or a bad person based on the evaluation by the PC people that are around you according to their understanding of the current list. They don't refer to a universal list of rights and wrongs, or to tried-and-true do's and don'ts, or to books that codify speaking and conduct based on centuries of experience. But there *is* a real desire to confiscate the personal freedoms of other people and condemn those who express disagreement with any of the things on their "current" PC list.

It you look for a definition of PC on the Internet, you will easily find the following universal explanation:

Political Correctness: conforming to a belief that language and practices which could offend political sensibilities (as in matters of sex or race) should be eliminated.[6]

On the surface, the definition doesn't seem to be particularly combative or strident. But in practice the list of *"matters"* is much longer than the two examples mentioned in the definition and for true Christians, the *"matters"* are not political. Rather, they are spiritual matters that pertain to morality and to life and death. Moreover, it is the intention of the PC people to impose their values upon the culture of America including in particular the part that pertains to the Christian community. Their unexpressed desire is for Christians to accept PC as a valid coexisting alternative to biblical morality aiming in the longer run to completely replace it.

Initially, the ideas on their List may sound interesting, maybe even moral or fair. But it always turns out that the tenets of PC are each a direct contradiction of a particular biblical principle or value. They are contemporary *"counterfeits"* of God's ways of doing things according to His Bible so that those who are rejecting the Word can feel better about themselves as they continue living in whatever way they want to outside of where the Light is. Therefore, PC is simply man's attempt to define morality for itself rather than submit to God .

As they pursue their own list of values, the PC folks like to challenge the Bible on several fronts. Sometimes they say the Bible was written by mere people who are subject to error, or that it was written many years ago and could not have foreseen the complexities of modern life, or that its message is being misinterpreted by ministers who have a political agenda or don't recognize the love (and related permissiveness) of Jesus.

This modern "enlightenment" refutes two thousand years of Christian understanding of foundational principles, many of which the Bible says about itself. One of those principles is that it was written under the direct influence of the Holy Spirit[7] even though some 40 people were chosen to do the physical writing of it. It says about itself that its principles and values are absolute[8] and like God they never change.[9] It says about itself that it is without error,[10] fully consistent[11] and complete in every respect.[12]

Those who challenge the Bible's meanings often base their assertions on their own *interpretations* of specific scriptures overlooking or disregarding the fact that their interpretations aren't consistent with the overall content of Scripture. You cannot challenge the Bible conclusively by relying on selected verses that out of context appear to support your point of view. *Everything* in the Word of God fits together into one complete aggregation called TRUTH that is totally void of contradiction.

Most true believers in Christ should be able to see with 20/20 spiritual perception that there is a Bible-related confrontation occurring all over our planet. Non-believers of course have trouble seeing it for what it is because they disregard the Bible as a credible source of information. The resulting challenge is for Christian believers to reveal the truth in love as a vital component of the work of the Body of Christ on the earth to make disciples of all nations.[13]

It is within this framework that the subject of administering the borders and boundaries of our nation has become contentious. On the surface it seems to be about whether or not to allow people who have come from other countries to enter and stay here after essentially ignoring standing immigration legislation and the will of the great majority of the people who are already living here legally. It seems also to be about the inability of our country to emerge from political paralysis and come up with lasting laws and policies that return us to order and the rule of law.

In actuality it is a spiritual issue. PC says that our country should take in any disadvantaged person who comes to our borders and that it is insensitive to refer to them as aliens or suggest that they are here illegally. They deny that political motivation is behind their idea of opening our borders insisting that it's their love and compassion driving them to advocate for the world's poor and hungry. However, the truth according to the Word of God is that the idea of nations having fixed and definite borders actually came *from* God. And as we will see in

Chapter 3, borders were, and still are, His idea keeping in mind that God never changes.[14]

A main purpose of this book is to call attention to the fact that the subject of borders and illegal immigration is simply a portion of a massive resistance to and hatred for the Bible just as Jesus described two thousand years ago. And now in these final days, the resulting confrontation has finally achieved a critical status all over the world. So far though, most Christians are reacting too passively to secularists and to a number of misdirected ministers as they try to justify a borderless world and circumvent our established immigration laws. When we hear some of them talk about compassion and love to defend their idea of opening our borders to unregulated migration, the true Church is essentially making, if anything, a political response instead of letting the world know what God has actually said about borders. Pastors don't preach about it because the subject is seen as too political which allows PC "love" to prevail.

Look! God doesn't deal in politics and the Church needs to do a better job of speaking out on His behalf from His Word. That's our job as Christians: to proclaim the Truth and we need to be a lot better at it than we have been so far. Let this book then remind you of the truth and motivate you to advocate for the Kingdom of God with passion and accuracy and urgency, in Jesus' Name!

*"I will have mercy on whom I will have mercy,
and I will have compassion on whom I will
have compassion."*

*Exodus 33:19(b)
Berean Study Bible*

Two:

Compassion and Christian Morality

Most people including many Christians jump to the conclusion that God has to be advocating for the borders of nations to be done away with. They see sensational pictures of the migrants on their television news and think that God must surely want the poor and the hungry people of the world to be admitted into our country of wealth and substance. After all, God is love[15] from which springs His unregimented mercy and compassion that is of a higher priority than any other thing. Moreover, borders divide people which surely must be antithetical to the plan of God for this planet. Surely, He wants to unite people!

It is, to say the least, often difficult to understand how and why God thinks the way He does and that's because we tend to make our assessments of Him based on our human ways of thinking and doing things instead of looking in His Word for clarification. Among other things, the Bible is a revelation of God's character along with His thinking and ways of doing things. It is patently unscriptural to assume attributes for Him beyond what we can substantiate in the Word. But there are those among us who speak what seems to be *"authoritatively"* about God's ways without having Scripture behind it which causes them and their audiences to come to the wrong conclusions. Others are expert at twisting what the Bible says to support some other agenda that has little to do with the Kingdom of God.

A few years ago, when the border issue had heated up under President Trump, I read an article in a major newspaper from a nearby town in which a local minister said that *compassion* for others is the defining characteristic of contemporary Christian morality. The context was about allowing all the *"refugees"* that can get here to enter into our country and that any idea to the contrary was simply unchristian for its lack of compassion *and* morality.

Now I too am a minister and I've been teaching Bible for a while. I don't know everything but from what I DO know, there isn't enough space in this book to explain all the ways that minister was biblically inaccurate in that longish, preachy article. Like so many in our culture today, he took a few scriptures out of context and created a “theology” to manipulate people to his point of view. In the process of doing that, he left out a lot of other scriptures that don’t agree with his conclusion and I don’t really know whether he did that from lack of knowledge or on purpose. As you will see, it could have been both!

In fact, as I continued reading his article, I eventually came to the apparent reason the minister was defining Christian morality for everyone: it seems that his ministry was receiving government grant money for all the migrants they could “minister” to and had come upon a time when they weren’t finding a sufficient number of new opportunities. Apparently, they were going to have to shut down if the then current level of border crossings didn’t open up again. For him, it was a crisis of Christian *immorality*!

Look, to know the will of God about a particular subject requires that we study His Word and find everything He said about it. All the statements about it have to be located, considered and then fit together to find His will. After that, we must be willing to accept what we find out whether it agrees with what we wanted it to be or not. As we will see in the next chapter, there are a number of scriptures that say that God Himself establishes the borders of all nations for His own special purposes whether we like it or not and whether we understand it or not. It's clearly there in Scripture and it is up to us to want to take the time to understand what the unalterable will of God actually is about this subject.

The Truth about Compassion

Human compassion for righteous causes is a good thing but its nature is personal. Righteous compassion is given by God to individuals. "Collective compassion" isn't in your Bible and what is also not in there is God's agreement for you to condemn others for not sharing your particular compassion. It also doesn't give you the right to confiscate the substance and money of others to use in the addressing of your personal compassion.

The Bible DOES say though that God is the One who defines morality, not human beings. The Ten Commandments did a good job of establishing a base line for morality and its statutes are plainly stated. There's no place where it says that a country must take under its care the poor people in the world for the sake of morality or for any other reason. In fact, the Bible doesn't even deal with immigration among countries. Furthermore, as we will see later, the words "stranger" and "sojourner" in your Bible have nothing to do with national immigration policy.

It also doesn't affirm "lawless compassion." Those who want to hold up unrestricted immigration as an issue of morality have no problem simply bypassing or ignoring the governing legislation of sovereign nations which clearly violates a multitude of other scriptures. Some say the laws are unjust, but can you find scriptures to back that up keeping in mind that the whole counsel of God must be considered? Compassion is not free to operate lawlessly unless it can be shown that the manmade law is unrighteous keeping in mind that unrighteousness is defined by God, not by people. *Not ever by people!*

Question: why would someone's compassion for unrestricted immigration be a higher moral priority than the security of our God-established borders and the welfare of our own people?

An Introduction to Christian Love

The other basic assertion is that Christian LOVE demands the giving of unrestricted access to the blessings that have been bestowed on America. For example, there are many people both inside and outside the true Body of Christ who say that Christians are bound by Scripture to open our borders and admit the world's migrants. We are to do this out of the *LOVE* for others that God commands us to demonstrate since after all God <u>*is*</u> love and Jesus *did* instruct us to love our neighbors, didn't He?[16]

There is a problem of understanding here and the truth is, the English word *"love"* is one of the most misunderstood words in the Bible. That's because there are four basic Greek words in the original text of the New Testament, each with a different meaning, that are translated into the one English word "love:"

Eros = physical, romantic and sexual love
Storge = love for family, kinship
Philia = love for friends, brotherly love
Agape = unconditional, sacrificial, God's love based on perfectly balanced mercy and justice

Was it not God Incarnate, LOVE Himself who on a number of occasions called the Pharisees a bunch of rather uncomplimentary names...*to their faces?*

Blind Guides[17]
Fools[18]
White-washed sepulchers full of dead men's bones[19]
Serpents[20]
Vipers[21]
Hypocrites[22]
Concealed tombs (for people to fall into)[23]

Was it not God Incarnate, LOVE Himself who drove the money changers out of the temple with a whip of cords that He had made with His own hands and turned over their tables in His anger against those who had turned God's *House of Prayer* into a *"den of thieves?"*[24] And was it not LOVE Himself who caused a flood to cover the planet that killed every living thing on it except eight people and a single boat-load of animals?[25]

In sum, people need to stop referring to the Bible as a source for justifying their personal concepts of compassion and morality until they know what it actually says. You need to know the context and it needs to fit in with all the other Scriptures once you have studied and understood the meanings of the original languages without having an agenda.

True bible-based love is sometimes "tough" love. It is not touchy-feely and it is not necessarily grounded in mercy and emotion. It DOES contemplate what is best for the one being loved and it DOES contemplate God's priorities even when they seem to go against the touchy-feely, emotional love that so many spiritually immature Christians think the Bible is talking about.

How would you react if you found out that in the mind and heart of God, what is best for the world's migrants is to never enter the U.S.? Stay tuned and find out!

"A day for the building of your walls! In that day the boundary shall be far extended. In that day they will come to you, from... sea to sea and from mountain to mountain."

Micah 7:11-12
English Standard Version

Three:

How God Views Borders

Without further discussion, let's find out next what God has actually said about borders free from the human agenda that so many try to impose on this subject. The truth matters and while it has not been widely taught, the Bible clearly says that God has definite and specific views on boundaries and borders. And, if the PC position leans towards *Open Borders*, you might expect God's position to be pretty much the opposite. That's exactly what Scripture confirms in the following foundational verses:

"From one man he made all the nations, that they should inhabit the whole earth; and he marked out their appointed times in history and the boundaries of their lands.

"God did this so that they would seek him and perhaps reach out for him and find him, though he is not far from any one of us."[26]

Notice first that these verses are in the New Testament (Acts 17:26-27). They confirm that the idea of having boundaries (borders) came from God and that He's the One who has set them all over the earth. He set them in the beginning and He resets them for appointed times according to His plans and purposes. We are all of the same ancestor, which is to say the same "blood," but God has divided us through the use of borders and boundaries for His own purposes. Let me repeat: God has Himself divided the peoples of the earth.

How do we know that God wants the people of the earth to stay divided? Also, are there some additional scriptures to confirm that God has always been the One setting the borders of nations?

Some Relevant Old Testament History

The answers to these questions start after the Great Flood as the three sons of Noah (Shem, Ham and Japheth) had children and began their genealogies. From the outset, God clearly told them to be fruitful and multiply and populate the entire earth abundantly.[27] The Bible shows that within about three hundred years of following these instructions, there were enough descendants that it came time for God to designate nations for them and each of those nations was given a designated area to inhabit with specific borders and boundaries. The Bible refers to this as the *inheritance of the nations* and at the beginning there were 70 designated nations:

Genesis 10:32 = *"These are the families of the sons of Noah according to their genealogies, and...out of these (descendants) the nations were separated on the earth after the flood."*

However, instead of going out to inhabit their inheritance, all the people of the earth came together in the land of Shinar and began to build a tower to heaven within a city that came to be called Babel. They resisted God's instruction to go out and populate the earth[28] and this reveals an important characteristic of fallen man: it is our nature to want to come together instead of separating out and into the nations to bring the Kingdom of God to the entire planet. Thus, it became necessary for God to *scatter* the people out from Babel to the areas He had assigned to accomplish His long-term plans and purposes:

Genesis 11:8-9 = *So the Lord scattered them abroad from there over the face of the whole earth..."*

After the *scattering*, the population of the earth gradually increased and when Moses came along almost 700 years later, the Lord had by then officially designated the descendants of Abraham to be His special people. As Moses led them out of Egypt and into the wilderness for 40 years, he reminded that it is God who establishes the borders of all the nations on the earth. He did that so the people would know that it is the authority of God that sets all the borders of the earth including the new ones they would one day receive in the Promised Land:

Deuteronomy 32:8 = *"When the Most High gave the nations their inheritance, when He separated the sons of man, He set the boundaries of the peoples…"*

At the end of those forty years in the wilderness and after the death of Moses, it became Joshua's assignment to lead the Israelites into the Promised Land. What transpired over the ensuing years was God's gradual reassignment of lands that had been originally designated for certain nations over to the twelve tribes of Israel, His chosen people.[29]

Some 500 years later, we find still another reminder during the reign of King David that it is God who sets the boundaries of the earth:

Psalm 74:17 = *"You (God) have established all the boundaries of the earth."*

The sum of this brief history is the clear confirmation that God has always been the One setting the boundaries and borders of the entire planet. And, He changes them whenever He wants to for His own purposes. To try to ignore those borders or rearrange them isn't part of man's job description. Borders serve God's purposes which are greater than we can understand and we tamper with them at our own risk. The idea of worldwide open borders is as clearly anti-God and anti-Bible as you can find.

Understanding Why God Wants Borders

Of course, we always want to know more precisely WHY God does what He does even though our little understandings of it are sure to fall way short of everything He has in mind. But we try anyway.

His initial purpose for having borders is to define the area of a *sovereign* entity. It is the means that God uses to bring order to the planet. Everything that God does is orderly and organized in every respect. Thus, a border sets apart a particular area where the people share common laws, beliefs, language, culture, governance, goals and objectives. Inside the border, there are agencies appointed to the tasks of protecting the inhabitants from outside intrusion and for regulating their activities according to local laws. It's a delegation of authority from God down through selected leaders to successively smaller groups for the same reasons that God later organized the Israelites.[30] God sets the borders and charges nations with the responsibility of defending the area that He has given them.

When the borders of nations are looked at this way, you can then notice that the Bible clearly says that God's overriding purpose is *so that mankind will be inclined to seek Him*. I'm not fully sure why it works this way but that is what the Bible says, so that makes it true. There's something about borders, a unique supernatural aspect to them, that makes people want to seek after God. Perhaps they more easily see the futility of trying to rule themselves on their own without God. Or they compare themselves to other nations where God is present and the people have benefitted from His presence.

Why have so many people wanted to immigrate to the U. S. since its founding? Is it not because we are a free people and because we are by far the most prosperous and powerful country in the history of the world? The United States has been given a unique role for the conversion of mankind to Christianity. For various reasons, borders help that process along. God is here, so prosperity is here, favor is here, opportunity is here and success is here. Indeed, all the benefits of God are here! Or, at least they're *perceived* from outside our borders to be available. People want to come here to participate in those benefits. But the Great Commission says we must go out to the nations.[31] Perhaps they can come here to be discipled but return to their home countries to carry out the Great Commission there. We can't accommodate all the people of the world who will want to come here. We are supposed to go there! Indeed, God wants us to defend our borders, the borders He has given us, so that people will reach out to Him from back in their own countries. Here are three key verses for you to keep in mind:

Matthew 28:18-20 = *"And Jesus came up and spoke to them, saying, 'All authority has been given to Me in heaven and on earth. Go therefore and make disciples of all the nations, baptizing them in the name of the Father and the Son and the Holy Spirit, teaching them* *to observe all that I commanded you; and lo, I am with you always, even to the end of the age.'"*

Mark 16:15-16 = *"And He said to them, 'Go into all the world and preach the gospel to all creation. He who has believed and has been baptized shall be saved; but he who has disbelieved shall be condemned.'"*

Acts 1:8 = *(Jesus said to His disciples), you will receive power when the Holy Spirit has come upon you; and you shall be My witnesses, both in Jerusalem, and in all Judea and Samaria, and even to the remotest part of the earth.*

He certainly does not want us to open our borders since doing that would in fact disrupt this process of God dealing with the nations. The disciples of Christ are supposed to go out to the nations to bring them the good news. They don't come here to receive it, we go there! This has been the plan for two thousand years. Who is mankind that we should think ourselves grand enough to tamper with it?

Who then would you suppose is the one behind the scenes trying to get rid of our borders? As always there is a spiritual Adversary involved. Open up the borders and you cancel a supernatural process to take the Gospel to the nations. That makes this an important topic for the Kingdom of God. Indeed, the Church of Jesus Christ needs to take notice of it. Only then can we stand up and protect the interests of both the Kingdom of God and the Church.

On the surface, the confrontation between open borders and defended borders is political. The world has made it that but it's actually a biblical issue. The politics of it isn't so much our concern but simply stated, the Democrat Party is the one that most loudly proclaims the idea of opening our borders and the Republican Party only knows to talk about the lawlessness and economic impact of it. Both parties are off track but Bible-believing Christians tend toward the Republican Party because directionally it tries to protect biblical values on a political level even as the Party itself finds new ways to divide itself over relatively small secular issues.

What is needed is for Christians to venture out from the political arguments about this subject and start speaking the truth from God's Word. What is especially needed is for Pastors around the country to bring the truth of this issue before their congregations so that the Body of Christ can be informed enough to advocate for the related Bible-based values and principles. If you are a Pastor, please go and preach it! If the Pastors don't preach the Word of God on these subjects, how will His people ever come to know the truth? From secular TV news broadcasts? God help us! If you are a lay person, study the Word and use this book as a guide to prepare yourself to speak the truth when you are presented with an opportunity. The Bible is pro-borders. God is pro-borders! Stand on the truth and be prepared to substantiate its position.

FORTY-THREE KEY SCRIPTURES ABOUT BORDERS IN CASE YOU THOUGHT GOD WASN'T INTERESTED IN THEM[32]

Psalm 147:14
He makes peace in your borders;
He satisfies you with the finest of the wheat.

Psalm 74:17
You have established all the boundaries of the earth;
You have made summer and winter.

Psalm 122:7
"May peace be within your walls,
And prosperity within your palaces."

Jeremiah 31:17
"There is hope for your future," declares the Lord,
"And your children will return to their own territory.

1 Chronicles 4:10
Now Jabez called on the God of Israel, saying, "Oh that You would bless me indeed and enlarge my border, and that Your hand might be with me, and that You would keep me from harm that it may not pain me!" And God granted him what he requested.

Malachi 1:5
Your eyes will see this and you will say, "The Lord be magnified beyond the border of Israel!"

Joshua 1:4
From the wilderness and this Lebanon, even as far as the great river, the river Euphrates, all the land of the Hittites, and as far as the Great Sea toward the setting of the sun will be your territory.

Deuteronomy 19:8
"If the Lord your God enlarges your territory, just as He has sworn to your fathers, and gives you all the land which He promised to give your fathers—

Isaiah 60:18
"Violence will not be heard again in your land,
Nor devastation or destruction within your borders;
But you will call your walls salvation, and your gates praise.

Proverbs 22:28
Do not move the ancient boundary
Which your fathers have set.

Isaiah 19:19
In that day there will be an altar to the Lord in the midst of the land of Egypt, and a pillar to the Lord near its border.

Exodus 23:31
I will fix your boundary from the Red Sea to the sea of the Philistines, and from the wilderness to the River Euphrates; for I will deliver the inhabitants of the land into your hand, and you will drive them out before you.

Deuteronomy 19:14
"You shall not move your neighbor's boundary mark, which the ancestors have set, in your inheritance which you will inherit in the land that the Lord your God gives you to possess.

Ezekiel 11:10
You will fall by the sword. I will judge you to the border of Israel; so you shall know that I am the Lord.

Jeremiah 15:13
"Your wealth and your treasures
I will give for booty without cost,
Even for all your sins
And within all your borders.

Numbers 34:12
And the border shall go down to the Jordan and its termination shall be at the Salt Sea. This shall be your land according to its borders all around.'"

Deuteronomy 32:8
"When the Most High gave the nations their inheritance,
When He separated the sons of man,
He set the boundaries of the peoples
According to the number of the sons of Israel.

Amos 1:13
Thus says the Lord, "For three transgressions of the sons of Ammon and for four I will not revoke its punishment, Because they ripped open the pregnant women of Gilead in order to enlarge their borders.

Jeremiah 17:3
O mountain of Mine in the countryside,
I will give over your wealth and all your treasures for booty, Your high places for sin throughout your borders.

Ezekiel 48:3
Beside the border of Asher, from the east side to the west side, Naphtali, one portion.

Numbers 15:38
"Speak to the sons of Israel, and tell them that they shall make for themselves tassels on the corners of their garments throughout their generations, and that they shall put on the tassel of each corner a cord of blue.

Numbers 34:3
Your southern sector shall extend from the wilderness of Zin along the side of Edom, and your southern border shall extend from the end of the Salt Sea eastward.

Ezekiel 27:4
"Your borders are in the heart of the seas;
Your builders have perfected your beauty.

Ezekiel 47:13
Thus says the Lord God, "This shall be the boundary by which you shall divide the land for an inheritance among the twelve tribes of Israel; Joseph shall have two portions.

Joshua 13:2
This is the land that remains: all the regions of the Philistines and all those of the Geshurites;

Isaiah 54:12
"Moreover, I will make your battlements of rubies,
And your gates of crystal,
And your entire wall of precious stones.

Ezekiel 11:11
This city will not be a pot for you, nor will you be flesh in the midst of it, but I will judge you to the border of Israel.
Numbers 34:10
'For your eastern border you shall also draw a line from Hazar-enan to Shepham,

Numbers 34:2
"Command the sons of Israel and say to them, 'When you enter the land of Canaan, this is the land that shall fall to you as an inheritance, even the land of Canaan according to its borders.

Micah 5:6
They will shepherd the land of Assyria with the sword,
The land of Nimrod at its entrances;
And He will deliver us from the Assyrian
When he attacks our land
And when he tramples our territory.

1 Chronicles 7:29
and along the borders of the sons of Manasseh, Beth-shean with its towns, Taanach with its towns, Megiddo with its towns, Dor with its towns. In these lived the sons of Joseph the son of Israel.

Malachi 1:4
Though Edom says, "We have been beaten down, but we will return and build up the ruins"; thus says the Lord of hosts, "They may build, but I will tear down; and men will call them the wicked territory, and the people toward whom the Lord is indignant forever."

Exodus 19:12
You shall set bounds for the people all around, saying, 'Beware that you do not go up on the mountain or touch the border of it; whoever touches the mountain shall surely be put to death.

Song of Solomon 1:11
"We will make for you ornaments of gold
With beads of silver."

Ezekiel 48:2
Beside the border of Dan, from the east side to the west side, Asher, one portion.

Micah 7:11
It will be a day for building your walls.
On that day will your boundary be extended.

Jeremiah 50:26
Come to her from the farthest border;
Open up her barns,
Pile her up like heaps
And utterly destroy her,
Let nothing be left to her.

Numbers 20:23
Then the Lord spoke to Moses and Aaron at Mount Hor by the border of the land of Edom, saying…

Joshua 18:12
Their border on the north side was from the Jordan, then the border went up to the side of Jericho on the north, and went up through the hill country westward, and it ended at the wilderness of Beth-aven.

Joshua 15:1-12
Now the lot for the tribe of the sons of Judah according to their families reached the border of Edom, southward to the wilderness of Zin at the extreme south.

Ezekiel 47:18
"The east side, from between Hauran, Damascus, Gilead and the land of Israel, shall be the Jordan; from the north border to the eastern sea you shall measure. This is the east side.

Ezekiel 47:15
"This shall be the boundary of the land: on the north side, from the Great Sea by the way of Hethlon, to the entrance of Zedad;

Numbers 34:6
'As for the western border, you shall have the Great Sea, that is, its coastline; this shall be your west border.

"...do not be conformed to this world, but be transformed by the renewing of your mind, so that you may prove what the will of God is, that which is good and acceptable and perfect."

Romans 12:2
New American Standard

Four:

The Problem of Wrongly Dividing Biblical Principles

Whenever a new PC tenet pops up, it comes with counterfeit rationalization. As already discussed, PC is man's attempt to replace biblical morality with a more "enlightened" code of conduct that seems righteous to unbelievers and to the secular culture. It attempts to replace biblical morality or discredit it or rearrange it. Of course, biblical morality is eternally, immutably absolute, but the world doesn't see it that way and is busily at work trying to discredit it.

People who oppose opening our borders are thus labeled as *xenophobic,* racist and as being blinded to the plight of people trying to escape political corruption and economic disadvantage. The truth is, we would love for many of those people to come into our country as long as we have an organized system of entry to protect the existing population and avoid anarchy. We are a country of laws and civil order that were originally based on biblical principles and the majority of Americans want our activities to continue along those same lines. It does NO good to anybody to admit new people only to have them immediately go on public financial support to the point they become dependent on it for the rest of their lives instead of on God. And, it's just plainly stupid to allow people in who want to kill us.

Along with the idea of opening the borders comes the seemingly compassionate justification for it and as usual, people who don't understand the Bible try to use it to present a righteous-sounding reason for what they want everybody to do:

Does the Bible not say that we should welcome and care for the "strangers" of the world?

The answer to this convenient interpretation is NO, the Bible does NOT say that in either the context of how the various nations conducted themselves 3,500 years ago or in the original Old Testament language of Hebrew. The truth is, the nations typically and vigorously defended their borders and required traveling groups of foreign people to obtain permission to enter into their domains. Foreign people from other nations respected those boundaries and as an example you can find in Scripture an example of the Israelites having to request permission from the King of Edom to enter his nation's territory as they were departing from the

Sinai.[33] And, you can also notice that the King refused permission and sent his army out against them which caused the Israelites to go another way. The basic idea here is that back in the day when the Old Testament was being experienced, foreign people had to request permission to reside in another country.

But how about smaller groups and traveling individuals? Indeed, this is where the various bible translations, particularly the most recent versions, have helped create confusion by being careless with their connection to key Hebrew words in the Old Testament. There are three Hebrew words in Scripture that need to be understood. A *"Ger"* was a person of foreign birth who had requested and obtained permission from Jewish officials to travel or reside within the borders of ancient Israel either temporarily or permanently. *"Ger"* can be translated into English as *sojourner*, *stranger* or *alien*. In Scripture the words *sojourner* and *stranger* carry the same meaning which is someone residing in Israel temporarily. If the visit became permanent, the word *alien* would be the better translation. A *Ger* as a non-citizen was to be treated with love and was subject to the same laws as a Hebrew citizen while they were in the country. They were to be paid as if they were Hebrews[34] and they were also expected to celebrate Passover,[35] observe Yom Kippur[36] and keep dietary and Holiness laws.[37]

But there are two other Hebrew words that apply to this discussion. The words *"Nekhar"* or *"Zar"* should be translated as the English word *foreigner* and a *foreigner* did not have the same rights and benefits as a *Ger*. A portion of the tithe was made available to help the *Ger* but not the *Nekhar* or *Zar*. If a Hebrew loaned money to a *Ger*, no interest was to be charged but it was okay to charge interest to the *foreigner*. If a visiting non-Hebrew didn't want to observe all the Jewish religious traditions, they would revert back to a *"Nekhar"* status where there were no particular benefits.

In sum, there is always a balance to these kinds of things in the Bible. People try to take a verse here or there out of context to back up their particular ideas which distorts its intention. What the Bible does say is that *"we are not to oppress sanctioned strangers or aliens who come among us,*[38] *we are to do no wrong or violence against them,*[39] *they are to be judged with the same laws as we judge ourselves*[40] *and we are to give them a fair hearing."*[41]

What it also says in the Old Testament is that the Jewish people should be individually hospitable to any non-Jew among them by providing them with temporary provision. It wasn't an instruction for the government of Israel or a requirement to open up their borders and let anybody come in without restriction. In fact, encouraging Gentiles (non-Jews) to come in and live among them was generally discouraged. But if some of them did come in, it was required that they be treated with the same laws and legal structure the Jewish nation already had for itself.

We should also look at a verse in the New Testament that open-border people like to cite:

"Do not neglect to show hospitality to strangers..."[42]

But they fail to consider that the previous verse sets the context as hospitality that is to be extended to fellow Christians who are sojourning strangers. Also, "hospitality" is a far cry from unrestricted and/or unlawful entry into a country for the purpose of taking up permanent residency. Scripture is to be taken as it is written and it is wrong to manipulate it for the purpose of deriving meanings that were never intended.

Just remember that the same God who establishes all the borders of all nations in order to maintain order and separation is the same One who gave instructions for how we should treat alien strangers who come among us. We have to consider the entire context of Scripture and most certainly it cannot be construed that the morality of a nation is only achieved by its willingness to throw open its borders to unrestricted entry. That idea is NOT Bible.

Indeed, the Great Commission says TO GO OUT and make disciples of all the nations.[43] It doesn't say to bring them all here and make disciples of them here.

Another way to see this might be that if the Church were doing a better job of carrying out the assignment of the Great Commission, many of the people who are presently clamoring to *"crash our gates"* would already be getting to know Jesus and would have learned by now how to bring God's blessing to their own countries. They wouldn't need to come here, and probably wouldn't want to!

In sum, I haven't found any instructions in my Bible that say America has a religious or moral responsibility for unrestricted admission of alien strangers into our country. It does NOT say to set up a welfare system of income redistribution so there will be money available to take care of all of them when they come into our country. It does NOT say we are to abandon our system of God-given bible-based law and order so they can freely come in at their option. And it does NOT say that we are to *cancel* the borders God has set up for the purpose of protecting our lawful citizens and providing a base from which the Gospel can be taken to the remotest parts of the earth.[44] As previously noted, the Bible does NOT even deal with the subject of immigration among sovereign countries.

One purpose of this book is to caution believers who aren't yet as mature in the Bible as they will hopefully be in the future. At first, the "values" we hear connected to PC ideas might *sound* good but they're NOT biblical. Being "inclusive," for example, sounds righteous, but there are many ideas and ways of living that God just isn't inclusive about. Being "loving" sounds righteous and I hear people, including even some Pastors, frequently reminding us to be more "loving" when we call attention to sin. But as we saw in the previous chapter, the love that the Bible mostly talks about isn't the same kind of love we usually think about when we're judging each other.

Bible love comes from the Greek word *agape* and it is the kind of love that God loves with. Regular human beings aren't even able to love that way unless we receive a lot of help from the Holy Spirit. Did Jesus love the Scribes and Pharisees when He was calling them "vipers"?[45] Yes, of course He did. And we have the same responsibility to call sin what it is, and agree publicly with what the Bible says it is, even if people don't like what we say.

That doesn't mean we don't love people. We love sinners and want them to be reconciled to God so they will be eligible for eternal life. We're even willing to be hated and called *xenophobes* and *homophobes* and other kinds of *"phobes"* if it benefits the Kingdom of God. There is NO sin ever committed that He is *unable* or *unwilling* to deal with. All He needs is a person who wants to turn away from it and come join His family. And how will they want to turn away if they don't hear the truth spoken to them?[46] Nevertheless, we DO want to talk about it as lovingly as possible keeping in mind that it's a judgment call and that there is a range of opinion on what constitutes "loving" speech. In the end, truth has to prevail and it will be either accepted or rejected. If "loving" speech has to avoid or twist the truth in order for it to be "loving," then it is no longer truth and you might as well keep silent. God's truth is supernatural and His love is contained in it. Who are we to judge the love of God and manipulate it to fit someone's human judgment of what is loving or not loving?

To conclude this chapter, there will always be inaccurate interpretations spewing out of unbiblical views of morality. The devil misquoted Scripture even to Jesus[47] and he continues to misquote and misrepresent it today. Any PC value or idea that comes up is guaranteed to have a truthful counterpart in the Word of God. The believer's job is to study the Word so we can bring attention to the truth and let it do its work on behalf of the Kingdom of God.

The same law shall apply to the native as to the stranger who SOJOURNS among you.

Exodus 12:49
New American Standard

Five:

What about the Refugees?

There is a tendency among the American Press to use the bible word *stranger* interchangeably with the non-bible word *refugee.* Suddenly, everyone coming from anywhere who wants to enter the U.S. is a *refugee-stranger* running away from something that somehow makes them eligible for American asylum, residency and financial support. They (the Press) either don't know that these two words have different meanings, or they're trying to mislead. It should not surprise if we discover that they actually *are* trying to mislead because historically most of them have been supporters of open borders as part of their never-ending sermonizing on what constitutes "correct" American conduct. Likewise, many of them, if not most, have become strangers to the truth. Therefore, a good way to start this chapter is by defining the word *refugee* and identifying some special aspects of it that are being misrepresented.

Refugees are people who have been forced to leave their country in order to escape war, persecution, or natural disaster.[48]

According to this actual English language dictionary definition, a refugee is not someone who has left their homeland voluntarily in response to economic hardship or inconvenience or based on personal desire to relocate, or in order to find a better job, or because they don't like their home country anymore or because they want to reconnect with family or friends who have already relocated.

Approximately ten percent of total annual legal immigration to the U.S. is comprised of actual refugees. Most of them are seeking asylum because of *persecution* and according to the law of the land, asylum for the reason of *persecution* has three essential requirements:

- First, applicants must establish that they fear persecution in their home/country.

- Second, they must PROVE that they will be persecuted on account of one of five protected reasons: race, religion, nationality, political opinion or particular social group.

- And third, applicants must establish that their governments are either directly involved in the persecution or unable to control the conduct of

> those individuals who are carrying out the persecution.[49]

Since World War II, more legal refugees have found homes in the U.S. than any other nation and more than two million have arrived here since 1980 out of a total of some twenty million legal immigrants. Nevertheless, and to repeat for emphasis, the word *refugee* is not a Bible word.

The Bible does say that a *stranger* is someone from some other country who has already come among the citizenry according to the entry requirements of the host country. God's people are encouraged to voluntarily and individually offer *temporary* accommodation and hospitality to *strangers*. How the *stranger* enters another country is not covered by Scripture. As already stated multiple times, the Bible does not deal with the subject of immigration among countries.

Despite this truth, I frequently hear or read where certain self-professing Christian teachers use selected Old Testament scriptures to define New Covenant morality. The argument goes something like this: *"The Bible shows us that Christian morality requires that we welcome strangers/refugees into our country without restriction if they are coming from less well-off countries and want to relocate to a place where they can live better lives."*

That idea is unscriptural at its base because Christians have been set free from the bondage of the Law of the Old Testament.[50] Even worse is when it's being misinterpreted out of context. Rather, Christian morality is defined by faith in Christ plus a willingness to submit to His ongoing Lordship on a day-to-day basis. Christian ministers and leaders who use Old Testament guilt and manipulation to pressure Christians into agreeing with their immigration agendas need to consider the entire Scripture on this subject. It takes faith and only faith to please God[51] and He's the same God who established the borders of the nations for His own purposes even though we don't fully understand it.

A Personal Testimony

I know from personal experience what refugees are and I know how they are different from other kinds of immigrants. I have actually lived in both situations and here is my testimony: I lived in Miami, Florida from June of 1978 until July 2012, a total of 34 years. Over those years more than one and a half million actual *refugees* from Cuba arrived in Miami fleeing Communist persecution, oppression, confiscation, political imprisonment and murder. They came to the U.S. and became successful *on their own* while they were helping turn a sleepy southern vacation town into a thriving economic and cultural center. There was essentially no restriction on the entry of Cuban refugees into the U.S. What they were seeking were freedom, safety and sanctuary!

During those same years I was also witness to the relocation of 250,000 people coming to South Florida from Haiti. They were not *refugees* because at the time they were mainly fleeing economic issues which made them unprocessed immigrants. They came mostly by boat and if they were intercepted off-shore they were sent back to Haiti. If they were able to set foot on U.S. soil, they were allowed to stay pending a legal review of their case, the same situation we have today. I never heard of any of them being sent back to Haiti and they became a part of Miami diversity because the U.S. basically extended amnesty to them instead of insisting on applying the law. Please don't misinterpret this: the Haitians are GREAT people and I love them. But they were not *refugees* according to the law.

After that, there came tens of thousands of "visitors" (aka sojourners) from South America and the Caribbean islands. They were given work visas, tourist visas, student visas, diplomatic visas and whatever other kind of visas the bureaucrats could think of. Those visas were supposed to be temporary because most of those folks were supposed to go back to their home countries. But when their visas expired, most of them just stayed in South Florida. And their relatives came and they stayed too. And now, the population of Miami includes many thousands of other wonderful people who have become U.S. citizens. None of them were *refugees* except the people from Cuba and perhaps some who were fleeing Communism in Venezuela.

There are people in the U.S. today including Christian clergy who want to open our borders and let in anyone who wants to be here. But they aren't fully considering what they are advocating. What happened in Miami is that so many people arrived in such a relatively short period of time that it was impossible to absorb them into the American culture. Many of the original immigrants never even had to learn to speak English and were never assimilated. Eventually there developed a unique hybrid culture which is certainly nice but it's not a typical American culture. Before we moved away after twenty years in the same office space, new Spanish-speaking arrivals were complaining because we wanted our ministry to continue operating in English instead of Spanish: "*who did we think we were trying to do business in Miami without operating in Spanish.*" If you go to Miami today you will find that it's a great place with a lot of wonderful people. But it isn't a typical American city even though perhaps it's slowly gravitating in that direction. It is, though, a unique city.

The point to be made is that based on the assumption that we want to preserve most of our culture, the admission of *refugees* and *stranger-sojourners* has to be intelligently managed and measured or our own people will be overtaken by a new culture they can't cope with. We can't just open our borders and frankly it's really naïve to be advocating it. We have had something special in America that people from all over the world want to come and be a part of. It would be folly to lose the very thing that has attracted them.

Some Economic Considerations Too

Something you may not have fully thought about is that widespread undocumented entry into this country causes regional economic hardship for our existing low-income workers. They are already here legally working hard and trying to support their families. The more *refugees* and *strangers* that come in, the more that low-income residents are negatively affected. They lose their jobs to the new refugees and undocumented aliens who are willing to do low-skill jobs for lower wages. Employers may like that but God who sets our borders apparently does not.

During my years in Miami, it was the African-American community that was most affected negatively by the influx of foreign labor. I watched them struggle until finally many were forced to move north and out of South Florida. Or just stay and go on welfare or get involved in illegal commerce. They complained about it but little was done. We needed to give refuge to the people coming from Cuba. But even more, we also needed to figure out a way to protect the wonderful people who had been living in South Florida for five or more generations.

Should we not be more compassionate in supporting and protecting our existing people as we are with the world's refugees? Those who clamor for open borders all the time are advocating policies that will severely damage the economic status of the weakest among us. People need to think these things through because whatever is attempted outside the wisdom and counsel of God will never lead to good conclusions. In God, we ought to be unified in concern for our own people as a first and highest priority.

Our Court system is presently over-whelmed by *strangers* coming into our country and requesting asylum. Only *refugees* are legally entitled to asylum and most of the people requesting it today are NOT entitled. They *should* be eventually denied but their cases have to be heard and officially decided at great cost to our taxpayers. There are presently more than a million pending court cases. If we do not soon return this entire process back to a prevailing legal structure, we are risking the institutionalizing of territorial anarchy that will ruin our country way more than it already has, perhaps irreparably This isn't a good time for Christians to be divided on such an important issue.

We can be kind, hospitable, welcoming and loving to strangers, sojourners, aliens and *refugees* without putting our existing residents at risk or negatively affecting their economics. The biblical concepts carry a connotation of *temporary* accommodation toward people who are passing through. All those who come in, whether temporarily or more permanently should submit themselves to our laws and we should not treat them differently than our existing residents. Not because I say so but because that is what the Bible actually says when we consider all of it instead of just the parts that make some people feel better about themselves when they haven't rightly divided God's intentions.

In sum, here are the main takeaways from this chapter: not anywhere close to all the attempted immigration going on today involves actual *refugees*. The United States is not required by Scripture and/or *"contrived morality"* to take any of them in. We do want to be a blessing and help some of them without destroying our own culture.

It is our underlying bible-based Christian culture that has made us exceptional because it flows out of God's presence. It's the thing that has brought His blessing to us, the same blessing that makes outsiders want to come here. But it's also what makes so many people hate us. They pursue our benefits without our Bible-based culture not realizing that it's impossible to do because the two things are inextricably joined together.

It should come as no surprise though that people who are less well off in the world should want to move to America. But we can't accommodate everybody. Just in the three countries of northern Central America (Guatemala, Honduras and El Salvador) there are almost 35 million people. Mexico has more than 100 million. They all need our help and if we choose not to accommodate them all here, there are other things we could do to help them.

One thing to consider is that the Church could do a better job of providing both spiritual and material solutions to all these people. How about policies that do a better job of monitoring the use of foreign aid to ensure that those funds are actually helping people? How about economic policies that encourage the development of private enterprise in these countries to provide jobs and income? How about law enforcement assistance to meet the challenge of the gangs and cartels? In sum, there are other ways to meet the needs that are driving desperate people to our borders. Illegal immigration is not the only way and it's not even the best way!

American Citizenship

This is a good place to emphasize that there is a legal way to immigrate to America and become a U.S. citizen in the same way millions upon millions of sojourner-stranger-residents have followed over many years. We are after all a nation of immigrants with borders that God has set for these Last Days and here are the *highlights* of the established entry process:

The first step is to apply for a work permit called a "Green Card." This can be done at the U.S. Embassy or Consulate in the applicant's home country. Immigration personnel there will explain the requirements for being considered. It can be helpful to have the sponsorship of a U.S. citizen. There will be a related interview and a following waiting period of typically six months to two years.

After taking up legal residency in the U. S. there is a path to becoming a citizen with the following basic requirements just for illustration purposes:[52]

- Be of the minimum required age (typically, at least 18)

- Continuously and physically live in the United States as a green card holder for 3 to 5 years

- Establish residency in the state or the U.S. Citizenship and Immigration Services (USCIS) district where you intend to apply

- Have "good moral character"

- Be proficient in basic spoken and written English and demonstrate knowledge of U.S. history and government

- Register for military service (for males age 18 to 26) and be willing to perform civil service when required

- Swear allegiance to the United States

By the Way

As a postscript for this chapter, before I moved to Miami, I lived for ten years in Central America as an executive employee of a large multinational corporation. Most of that time was in San Salvador, the capital city of El Salvador. Over those years I traveled to all of the countries in the area hundreds of times and traveled into the interiors of Guatemala, Honduras, Belize, El Salvador, Nicaragua, Costa Rica and Panama. I had and still have MANY Hispanic friends from those countries and love them more than I can express in this book.

While I was living there, I helped several people immigrate to the U.S. by providing local endorsements and references through the local American Embassy which was, and still is, the legal way to immigrate to the U.S. In those days it took about two years of waiting but when the approvals came, those people came here and never had to give it a second thought. They were here legally creating a testimony of American generosity and history as they busily assimilated into our American culture.

I also had the satisfaction of making it possible for a bean-farmer, gardener-friend to become the first landowner in the history of his family over ten generations. He had been trying all his adult life to accumulate eight hundred dollars in order to purchase two hectares of land (approximately five acres) that he had farmed for twenty years via an interest-only privately-held and annually renewed mortgage that required the full asking price in a single payment to purchase the property outright.

You should also know that I speak fairly fluent Spanish and you might want to keep this little section in mind when you are getting ready to call me a racist or a xenophobe. Those would not be accurate labels according to either the definitions in Webster's Dictionary or to actual demonstrated experience. I know that truth still matters to some people and certainly it matters to God. Read what the Word says and throw out any of your opinions and values that disagree with what it actually says.

"The fear of the Lord is the beginning of knowledge; but the foolish despise wisdom and instruction."

Proverbs 1:7
English Revised Version

Six:

A Scarcity of Wisdom

There was a time in America when we were a lot wiser than we are now. I'm speaking of the whole country because there have always been the unwise among the wise. But over the 245 years of our existence as a country (as of 2021), the influence of wisdom that was once so powerful has gradually dwindled and given way to the preeminence of poor judgment, naiveté and just plain foolishness.

For purposes of this book, let's establish this following definition:

Wisdom is the ability to apply one's knowledge in a way that consistently produces good judgments.

The wise person has the ability to form opinions objectively and make decisions that turn out to be the most beneficial ways of taking action. Things just turn out right. They have an understanding of the factors that need to be considered to produce the best outcomes. Sometimes it's even called common sense or innate intelligence. But the truth is, ALL authentic wisdom comes from God and the successful use of it has been rooted in centuries of related experience and knowledge.

The Bible talks extensively about it and calls it the principal thing one can acquire.[53] The Apostle Paul prayed that believers in the church of Ephesus would acquire a spirit of wisdom so they could be enlightened to the things of God they had inherited.[54] The Bible also says that fools despise wisdom because they refuse to accept the instruction of God[55] that's necessary for wisdom to even exist. To repeat: all true wisdom comes from God. People on their own are incapable of generating true wisdom.

So, let's understand the situation: we started out in 1776 with a group of some of the wisest people who ever lived. Despite what secular historians refuse to acknowledge, almost all our founding fathers were Christian believers with advanced knowledge and understanding of the Bible who had personally experienced the *First Great Awakening* (1730-1755). They wanted to put together a new type of government that advocated and protected a condition of freedom for its citizenry. They understood that all true freedom also comes from God[56] and not from the governments of men.

Actually, it's the nature of men to restrict freedom so we can control others for the purpose of fulfilling our own agendas. That's why our founding documents embrace and emphasize the presence and influence of Almighty God in both life and government.

Many of those wise founders confirmed in their personal writings the understanding that the success of their revolutionary experiment fully depended upon the ongoing influence and involvement of God. It was never their intent that God be separated from governance because they knew by the wisdom of the Bible that true freedom cannot exist without God's presence.

So, we started out operating with Him at the forefront, close at hand. Not everything was perfect because nothing that mankind ever does is perfect. Sin and flesh get in the way. But the presence of God provided a direction for working toward the correction of those things that weren't right yet. But, take God out of the loop and we will ALWAYS lose our way. Things don't happen right anymore; wrong decisions are made. Wisdom is lost.

Over time people have gradually stopped reading their Bibles, stopped going to church, stopped praying and stopped honoring the Holy Spirit. And finally, on June 25, 1962 the Supreme Court decided that a prayer approved by the New York Board of Regents for use in their public schools violated the First Amendment because it represented an establishment of religion. The next year, it cited the same reasoning in deciding against Bible reading as well completing the process of effectively expelling the Lord God Almighty from our public-school systems across the country.

Since that time, studies clearly show that academic performance has nosedived. Take God out of the equation and people will always go in the wrong direction. In this case, true knowledge has decreased. With less knowledge there is less understanding. And, with less understanding there is less wisdom which is directly connected to the presence of God. As of the year 2021, we have 58 years of relatively God-free public education and the result is a severe shortage of real wisdom all over our country. Unfortunately, it's getting progressively worse. Would you have imagined even a couple of short years ago that many of our public schools would be indoctrinating children with the idea based in Marxist ideology that our entire legal system needs to be overhauled because all this time it has been racist? Read up on *Critical Race Theory* and see what you think. You need to be informed about these things or your lack of knowledge will eventually kill us![57]

When I was writing the original book on this subject, the country was getting ready for the mid-term elections in November 2018. Suddenly, there appeared as a "serious" topic for political discussion one of the least-wise ideas ever conceived up to that time by our burgeoning contingent of the unwise: let's seriously consider doing away altogether with the government agency that regulates the entry of new people into our country. By doing that, it was thought that *"unfair pressure"* on existing and already present undocumented aliens would be reduced and that eventually we could get to a place where we would have no immigration controls and just allow folks to come and go as they please. There are significant economic and political consequences connected to this idea but the larger responsibility of protecting existing domiciled and legal citizens of the U.S. from non-vetted aliens is lower on the list of priorities.

Following that brilliant idea, there has come behind it the unbelievably stupid notion of reducing the presence of law enforcement in America. Militant groups of *"occupation"* have taken over control of some of our cities and crime is soaring. Indeed, wisdom is rapidly disappearing from the American culture because people have decided to eradicate God from it as much as possible. When the presence of God decreases, both wisdom and freedom go with Him. Said another way, as God is reduced stupidity and bondage take His place.

While President Trump was in office (until January of 2021), the problem of illegal migration had been largely controlled by some brilliant strategic interaction with several related countries. The crisis at our southern border had seemingly been solved.

We expected it to be solved and who would have ever thought that opening our borders would have become a serious consideration here anyway. But what were your first thoughts when someone mentioned the idea of biological males being allowed to use the intimate facilities of biological females? Or, I wonder what the first thoughts of Christian folk back in 1963 were when somebody came up with the *"brilliant-idea"* of kicking Christian prayer out of the public-school System. In sum, what we are seeing now in our culture is the result of a growing scarcity of wisdom as the country moves farther and farther away from God. And the truth is, the decline is accelerating.

The serious consideration of opening our borders is part of that decline and the Church needs to see it for what it is. And by the way, it isn't something new. We're just finally noticing something that's been flying under the radar for a while. Actually, for quite a while, about 150 years! But finally, it's coming out in the open and it's an unbiblical, unwise idea which makes it just the thing now for PC to adopt as one of their key tenets! In fact, we are likely to be dealing with the border issue for a long time to come, because while we were sleeping, it became something way bigger than we ever thought possible.

Indeed, within a fortnight following the inauguration of the new administration after President Trump, the essence of wisdom departed and fools again rule the day. Already in the first months of 2021, we are being invaded by thousands of unvetted people of foreign origin as fools look on wondering what all the fuss is about:

Proverbs 9:10 = *Reverence for God is the foundation (the beginning) of wisdom and understanding comes from knowing Him.*

I end this chapter with the most relevant and compelling scripture I could find. If God ceases to be important to a culture, if the culture ceases to honor the One who set our borders and called us to the Great Commission, then wisdom will decline and the ability to make good judgments extinguished. At some point God will either bring us a revival or go find some other country where wisdom still reigns and the people want to finish the job of establishing His Kingdom on the earth.

*"When the Most High gave to the nations
their inheritance, when he divided
mankind, he fixed the borders
of the peoples according
to the number of the
sons of God."*

*Deuteronomy 32:8
English Standard Version*

Seven:
A Brief History of Open Borders

Let's start this chapter by defining what we're calling *Open Borders* so we can all be considering the same idea. This is not my definition; it's how the serious open border people define it and it's actually what they want the world to become.[58] An open border is a boundary of a sovereign political jurisdiction where free movement of people is allowed with no restrictions. In other words, there's no meaningful or substantive border control involved. People are free to come and go as they please without restriction.

Now in performing research for this book, I found that there are a number of publications on the Internet to "document" just about anything somebody would want to say about this subject. I've tried to be careful in considering these things so I could come away with the truth. People on both sides of the debate are emotional about what they believe and not surprisingly seem to select and arrange their "facts" to line up with their agendas. I hope I have filtered through their various biases even though admittedly I also have an agenda based on the interests of the Kingdom of God.

The open border folks want us to believe that prior to 1924, the borders of the United States were open. According to their own definition, that is not true. The truth is, quota-based immigration laws were formalized in 1924. Prior to that, there have always been restrictions of some kind dating back to the *Naturalization Act of 1790*,[59] revised in 1795 in response to anti-immigration pressure.[60] In 1798 the *Alien Friends Act* first authorized the President to deport any resident immigrant considered "dangerous to the peace and safety of the United States."[61] And since then, there has indeed occurred unrestricted and unrecorded immigration into the U.S. but that's because it was impossible to police our lengthy borders. The idea of opening them up to unrestricted immigration has never been the policy of this country nor has it ever been the desire of the majority of our people. We *have* been sympathetic to the ongoing admission of new immigrants for both economic and humanitarian reasons as long as it was generally an orderly process and beneficial to the country's objectives. Since that original Naturalization Act, there have been more than 40 enactments of federal legislation that served to establish rules of immigration and citizenship.[62]

In the beginning of America, the individual states (rather than the Federal government) had the responsibility for hands-on immigration regulation. Eventually, the major entry point became the immigration station known originally as Castle Garden operated by the State of New York from 1855 to 1890. Approximately eight million immigrants passed through its doors.[63] What would you suppose state immigration officials were doing there? They were performing the required inspection and registration of arriving immigrants. Does that sound like an open border to you based on the definition in the first paragraph of this chapter?

Then in 1890, President Benjamin Harrison designated Ellis Island to be our first federally operated immigration station and it eventually started up on January 1, 1892. More than twelve million immigrants passed through that single-entry point during its sixty-two-year life. What were they doing there? They too were inspecting and registering immigrants.

In fact, the federal government set up a formal inspection process at Ellis Island and here's how it worked between 1892 and 1924. First and second-class passengers arriving in N.Y. Harbor received an initial inspection aboard ship. Unless they were found to be sick or with legal problems, they were allowed to disembark, pass through Customs and then enter the U.S. after a proper registration of their arrival. If they did have legal problems, they were sent to Ellis Island for a more complete investigation.

The process was more rigorous for third class passengers. Their ships would dock at the Hudson or East River piers and those folks were then transported by ferry or barge directly to Ellis Island where everyone underwent medical and legal inspections.[64] If any of them were unable to demonstrate that they could be reasonably expected to provide for themselves financially, they were sent back to their country of origin. Does this sound like an open border policy to you where everybody could travel back and forth however they wanted to?

The sum is this: present-day open border people in the U.S. are trying to get us to believe the idea that this country has historically had an open border policy and that we should now *return* to that way of operating. At the same time, they want us to agree that it's historically un-American and immoral to now come up with measures that put restrictions on immigration for the purpose of protecting the safety of Americans who're already here. The truth is, we have never been an open border country and polls show that the great majority of people living here today legally do not want open borders.

Nevertheless, if you are against open borders then you are "diagnosed" as suffering from *xenophobia*. That is the default designation for all people who disagree with their way of thinking. However, the official and accurate definition of *xenophobia* applies to folks who have an *irrational* fear of people from other countries. Is it irrational to want to vet applying immigrants to find and weed out the ones who hate us, who reject our form of democratic governance and who have sworn publicly to kill and overrun us? Have we ever had such people enter the country? If you possess even a little of God's wisdom, you will be able to answer these questions correctly. In fact, many of the folks who call us *xenophobic* are the same ones who hire armed body guards and build walls around their own houses for fear of the growing lawlessness prevailing in their local communities.

The actual history of this country is a generosity that features orderly immigration with open arms, not open borders. But here is a key point to consider: what should our history have to do with determining what our current immigration policies should be? The administration of our borders today should be formulated in the context of today's environment which includes instant communications, prolific social media usage, worldwide political and economic unrest, militant religious groups, hatred of the supporters of Israel, nuclear capability of sworn enemies, global transportation, foreign gangs and drug cartels, etc. Today's environment for regular people is vastly different than it was in 1798 or 1890 or 1924. The point of trying to use history, even their revised/fake history, to rationalize open borders for America today is without relevance!

Have we lost so much wisdom that we would now open our borders to the world's lawless, allow them to come in and out as they please with little regard for the welfare of our law-abiding citizens and residents? Or for their wishes? Why would any rational people in this day and age consider such ideas?

Yes, I used the word *lawless* in the previous paragraph because the millions of aliens who have circumvented the immigration laws that we actually *do* have on the books and are living here illegally are by definition law-breaking and therefore *lawless*. There's a legal immigration process available and they chose to ignore that process and enter the country illegally with the aid of self-serving politicians and employers aided by a feckless Congress.

Someday the enablers will have to explain things to God. That is the same God who established all our borders so that people would reach out to Him and so order could be maintained on the planet. Have you noticed that where unrestrained migrations have broken out such as in Western Europe that widespread pandemonium and *DIS*-order have consequently prevailed? Meanwhile there's a demonic influence behind this push for open borders that we need to deal with…so keep reading!

Who is wise? Let them realize these things. Who is discerning? Let them understand. The ways of the LORD are right; the righteous walk in them, but the rebellious stumble in them.

Hosea 14:9
New International Version

Eight:

The Real Reasons They Want Open Borders

When I started studying this subject, I didn't realize how much I didn't know. For one thing I had not fully connected biblical scripture to the idea that God is the One who likes borders the most. I had looked at open borders in a political sense and had concluded that the people who wanted them were pretty much intellectually unconscious. What they wanted to do just didn't make sense from the standpoint of public safety not to mention the negative economics of it.

I *had* noticed that it seemed to be increasingly a position of the Democrat Party which made me suspicious even though I try not to look at cultural issues through just a political lens. But the truth is, the two parties are roughly equal in member registrations. So based on history, it wouldn't be unexpected for either or both of them to be interested in increasing their respective voter registrations in order to get control of more votes for the future.

I don't want to believe that there really are people who would put the interests of their political parties ahead of the interests of the United States. But then, I happened to notice that certain of the leaders in that particular political party who are known to favor socialist ways of doing things had become the most vocal about open borders. I thought perhaps it was because they hated the then President (Trump) so much that they had just turned up their screeching a bit louder. But it had gotten my attention and I decided to look into it more deeply.

I found out that the idea of open borders coming to America goes back to the nineteenth century well before Ellis Island. As you might expect, there was originally the usual European influence that contributed to people starting to talk about it over here. Eventually that all led to the *International Emigration Conference* of 1924 in Rome where it was decided that everybody should have the right to travel or immigrate to any country they want to without restriction. Interestingly, that's the same year the United States officially implemented its new quota system control on immigration. And since then, there has been a continuous undercurrent in the U.S. for a *"return"* to open borders accompanied by a gradual tendency in that direction.

The United Nations is officially in favor of open borders, and it has been for decades. Its present Secretary General is an avowed Socialist from Portugal. According to information on the Internet, the U.N. applies continuous pressure all over the world for countries to move toward the elimination of their borders and immigration controls. Ostensibly it's for the purpose of discouraging "hyper-nationalism," but without borders the world winds up someday with one big entity called the United Nations that presumably would have authority to govern/rule everybody on the planet.

Did you know that there is an *Open Border Manifesto*[65] out there among the nations? It's supported by various U.S. political organizations, agrees in detailed principle with the United Nations and reveals the real reason we have such pressure to relax border controls. At the root of this movement is a clearly stated *involuntary* redistribution of wealth from the countries that are the most economically blessed to the majority that are poor. It ignores the biblical truth that God has set borders and boundaries for His own purposes. And, it would redistribute wealth away from those who would use it to take the Gospel to the nations so that God Himself can be the One to lead them out of their poverty.

This is why American Socialists support open borders: they want to be with the group that's in charge of redistributing the wealth. After all, if wealth is to be redistributed, somebody has to be in charge of making that happen. Somebody has to take over control of the regulation and use of all that wealth. Who will that be?

In the meantime, the political party that embraces these interests needs more voters because the traditional American republic and its Church stand in the way of this giant one-world take-over. Surely it is particularly ironic that the political party that most supports abortion in America falls short of the votes it needs to take over things? Over the years they've aborted their own future constituency and now don't have enough votes to overwhelm their opposition and carry out their agenda. As a result, they now must resort to supporting the entry of illegal aliens and to other acts of vote manipulation to elect their candidates and maintain control.

What's wrong with Socialism?

There was a time not so long ago when we didn't have to ask this question, when the great majority of Americans had an informed aversion to it. They knew it was counter-cultural and an inferior economic system. Indeed, the American culture has always been based on individual freedom under God. Socialism is a failed secular collective system that restricts individual freedom in order to benefit the collective. It is the antithesis of the free enterprise system that along with trusting God has made us the most exceptional country in the history of the world. But more people today with their increasing lack of wisdom are seriously considering socialism as a viable alternative to our traditional way of life.

One major reason socialism will never succeed is that it is rooted in *covetousness* which is a bible term defined as an inordinately strong envy with a related desire to acquire somebody else's substance. It is mentioned in the New Testament as a major form of unrighteousness that disqualifies an individual from being able to inherit the Kingdom of God.[66]

The complaint heard most often about capitalism is that it creates a disparity of income between ownership and labor. Socialism wants everybody to be the same but when it has been tried, no one will venture into ownership because the risk isn't sufficiently rewarded. Government is always eager to provide ownership but it will never function efficiently which is why socialism always collapses. And anyway, Jesus clearly taught that because of differences in ability among individuals, there will always be naturally occurring economic disparity.[67]

Capitalism by definition requires the free exercise of commerce, and as we now know, freedom is something that comes only from God. But for capitalism to work at maximum effectiveness, the risk-taking owners must be submitted to God and to biblical principles of life and finances. Without God in the mix, ownership will almost always wind up taking a disproportionate share of the profits because of greed which is just as ungodly as covetousness. The bottom line is that the best system of commerce has proven to be a free one involving God and an ownership that is led by biblical principles and the Holy Spirit. Nevertheless, even when biblical principles are compromised, a free economic system will always out-perform other systems where bondage and involuntary wealth distribution are involved.

In sum, socialism is a system that God will never be involved in because it directly violates biblical principle which is why the PC folks now like it even if they don't realize it.

What about Globalism?

The whole world is talking about *globalism* these days and it's an issue that is directly related to the subject of our *borders*. It is defined as the idea of placing the interests of the entire world (the globe) above those of individual nations. Since individual nations are defined by God's borders and boundaries, *globalism* disregards those boundaries based on the thinking that a world with common interests will operate better and in more harmony than a world divided by borders.

Over the years the idea of globalization has been increasingly supported by America. We entered into trade agreements that benefited other countries more than the U.S. We provided disproportionate finances to prop up the United Nations, NATO and various other organizations around the world. We provided foreign aid and didn't complain when many of the recipient countries failed to support us politically and even actively worked against us.

Western Europe has tried globalism through a Common Market that has had a lot of problems. In fact, the idea of unrestricted immigration has decimated major cities in Germany, Belgium, France and the United Kingdom. Globalization failed to head off terrorism and if anything helped promote it proving that wisdom is on the decline everywhere.

In 2008 the US elected a Progressive President who is a globalist. He promised to change American culture. For eight years globalism was championed and promoted and affirmed while we officially apologized for American exceptionalism. After all, it was the moral thing to do because the world was/is not as well off as we are which occurred because of a freak accident nobody can explain and despite the fact that we are really terrible people. Thus, we should spread our wealth around so the rest of the world will think better of us.

In 2016 we elected a President who had decided to champion nationalism over globalism by putting America first and the reaction was nothing short of tumultuous. The idea of putting our own country first, ahead of the interests of the rest of the World's countries goes against everything Progressivism with its borderless world order had been nurturing outside the wisdom and plan of God. That's why globalism won't work, and it never will work. If God has set the borders of the world for His purposes, globalism will always be an inferior alternative. And so, the new administration elected in 2020 with the resumption of a globalist agenda will be working against the will and plan of God for a planet of nations that are divided by borders. That is a dangerous strategy because the Bible says that God will not be mocked![68] The people of the world are to be divided geographically separated by borders even as they become united in Christ and that is precisely what will eventually come to pass.

What about Multiculturalism?

Another term that's thrown around these days is *multiculturalism*. It's a really complicated sounding word so most people just gloss over it intending to think about it later when they have more time. The majority of us don't ever get enough time so if you are paying attention now, it's defined as the idea that the American culture is strengthened by mixing it with a diversity of other cultures, the more the better. It's advertised to reduce cultural ignorance and division. But at what cost?

The possible cost is the dimming of the American culture that people immigrated here to take advantage of. When they left their home countries, there was something about their original culture that seemed less attractive than what they wanted to look for in America. Until recently, newcomers worked hard to learn English and become a part of our culture, to identify with it instead of the culture they had left behind. Now they are encouraged to stay with their original culture so it can change what we have wanted our country to be for generations.

At the end of the discussion, *multiculturalism* is little more than a disguise for unrestricted immigration that identifies with unrestricted borders. It is a rationalization that wants to convince us that ordered and intelligent immigration is less desirable than mixing all of the cultures of the world together into a single, random pot to be stirred by the few people who are smart enough to oversee everybody. *Maybe then God wouldn't be such a problem!*

Some amount of diversity may be a plus for our culture but no one knows how much that should be before we hit a point of diminishing return. What we do know is that every true Christian should be standing actively against the idea of open borders. That includes any of us who have supported illegal immigration in the past to attract and make use of low-cost alien labor. We need to put the Kingdom of God first in all things and that requires us to set aside our personal agendas because open borders are bad for the Kingdom of God. Unrestricted access to our country is outside the wisdom and counsel of God. It is also not Bible no matter what we try to call it. Therefore, it's bad for our country! In fact, that's part of the reason so many Christians supported former President Trump which is the subject of the next chapter.

The Authority… is a minister of God, an avenger who brings wrath on the one who practices evil.

Romans 13:3-4
New American Standard Version

Nine:

Why Bible-Based Christians Supported President Trump

Secular people had a problem understanding why true believers in Christ supported President Trump. In fact, analysis shows that the election of Donald Trump as President on November 8, 2016 happened because Evangelical Christian voters turned out in unprecedented numbers. Finally, the true and silent Christian majority got out of their passive, do-nothing, disinterested, above-the-fray, La-Z-Boys™ to make a statement on behalf of the Kingdom of God.

Sometimes President Trump didn't appear to act very Christian or religious. He cussed sometimes and seemed to get offended a bit easily. There was a weekly scandal about his past involving some un-Christian things he may have done. He wasn't as gentle or humble or caring as some would have liked. He called people names and disrespected them to the point that it was said about him that he *"took no prisoners."* In short, he seemed to be a person that would not appeal to the Body of Christ. So, what *was* his appeal?

One major thing that secular people fail to understand is that Bible-based Christianity isn't a political persuasion. It's about a personal relationship with our Creator that only a true believer can be involved in. It's about the coming together of believers under a fundamentally common agenda and purpose. The common purpose stems from a common assignment called the Great Commission conferred on us by God to pursue the discipling of the world's nations as discussed back in Chapter Three.

Jesus Himself spoke the assignment to us in the form of a command for what He wants the Body of Christ to do while we wait for His return. Meanwhile, the Adversary is fully purposed to impede our pursuit of this assignment as much as the true Church is dedicated to the idea of carrying it out. In recent years leading up to the Trump candidacy, we had even seen our own government working against the fulfillment of the Church's assignment. And, that's why Evangelical Christians finally turned out to vote for Candidate Trump. In his campaign he said repeatedly that when elected he would support the cause of the American Church instead of working against it. His opponent on the other hand made it equally clear that she would continue the former persecution.

Candidate Trump also assured that he was/is a Bible-believing Christian. Credible Christian leaders agreed publicly that he had made a true profession in which case his past-life experiences became irrelevant to the true believer. In fact, the top priority for the true believer was and still is to see the Kingdom of God established on the earth with everyone in all the nations having had a fair opportunity to accept or reject Jesus Christ as Lord. Donald Trump was the candidate who most identified with this priority. We may not like the way he talks sometimes and we may have wished that he would run his tweets by us before he released them, but those things were less important, less urgent considerations. It's not ever going to be about a President's personality or likeability. For the true Christian, it's about the Kingdom of God and about the Church of Jesus Christ

Close after that first priority was that the President was/is pro-life. The Body of Christ is pro-life because the Bible is pro-life. In fact, the Word of God clearly establishes that life begins at conception. Therefore, most true Christians will ALWAYS support candidates who are pro-life because abortion is clearly and categorically unrighteous. There is no bible-based way to compromise on this issue because it is about the lives of defenseless human beings. It is not a political issue, it's a moral issue of life or death. And so, the President's public support for life covered a multitude of shortcomings regarding his personality and ways of speaking.

Another of the President's priorities that attracted evangelical Christians was that he is strong for the protection and welfare of Israel. The roots of Christianity are in Israel and the true Church of Jesus Christ has taken upon itself the responsibility of supporting and protecting the nation of Israel, which also has God-set borders. It is presently a secular nation and the majority of its people have so far rejected their Messiah, but those details have nothing to do with obeying God's instructions to support Israel. It was Candidate Trump who made the strongest case for the support of Israel and that stance resonated with the Church.

The Body of Christ also saw that President Trump was determined to protect the borders that God has set for this country and in doing that protect the people who live here legally. Whether by a wall or check points or electronic surveillance or enforcement of existing legislation or introducing new legislation, he had stated his commitment to controlling immigration responsibly so that we are never left without borders. Christians will almost always be drawn to the support of borders and to the rule of law.

These are critical ideas because if we ever open our borders, we will cease to be a nation, and if we're no longer a nation, we would cease to be the place that other nations look to for God. Somehow, according to Scripture, our borders are a supernatural confirmation of His existence and it would be best for the secular folks of this world to steer clear of disturbing the things that are important to someone who was able to create the universe simply by speaking it into existence. That's just my advice for folks who're so interested in open borders and unrestricted migration. Even though Trump is gone, you may want to think this border thing through a bit more! You have God to contend with and as already pointed out, He will not be mocked.[69]

"He (God) sets up walls and ramparts for security."

Isaiah 26:1
New American Standard

Ten

What about the Wall?

The U.S. shares two long borders: one with Mexico to the south and the other with Canada to the north. Also, Alaska shares a border with Canada. This chapter focuses on the border with Mexico which is 1,954 miles long excluding the maritime boundaries that go into the Pacific Ocean and the Gulf of Mexico. Ostensibly, the current boundary was set by the *Boundary Treaty of 1970* as agreed to by Mexico and the United States. But as we now know, Scripture says the boundaries of nations have been set by God. And, what a lot of folks may not know about this particular boundary is that <u>it's the most frequently crossed border in the world</u> even if we just count the documented crossings of more than 350 million per year.[70] Only God knows what the real number is!

There are four states along the U.S. side of this border. From east to west, they are Texas, New

Mexico, Arizona and California. On October 26, 2006, President George W. Bush signed into law the *Secure Fence Act of 2006* that called for the construction of various specified "fences" along approximately 700 miles of the border. As he signed it into law, the President said,

"This bill will help protect the American people. This bill will make our borders more secure. It is an important step toward immigration reform."[71]

The passage of this legislation was a bi-partisan event initiated in the *House of Representatives* by NY Republican Peter T. King, passed there by a vote of 283 to 138 followed by passage in the Senate 80 to 19. There were 24 Democrat Party yea votes[72] in the latter including Senators Obama, Schumer and Clinton.[73] As they were preparing to vote, Senator Obama said the following:

"The bill before us will certainly do some good. It will authorize some badly needed funding for better fences and better security along our borders and that should help stem some of the tide of illegal immigration in this country."[74]

At the time, there was widespread agreement that the wall (aka fence) would make the border more secure by reducing both drug trafficking and unregistered immigration. Those were the mutually recognized security concerns stemming from the realization that people who want to hurt this country and kill Americans could easily cross the border with the regular flow of other undocumented aliens. Unfortunately, what was once bipartisan agreement soon broke down. Two years later, President Obama decided to support the opposite position of *Senator* Obama and so, lacking presidential support, the legislation was never fully enacted and never funded.

Ten years after the *Fence Act of 2006* was passed, the American people elected a President with an agenda that made sense. Included in it was the construction of a Wall (aka Fence) at strategic points along the southern border. Everyone knew very well that the purpose of the border Wall despite contrary political rhetoric was not to stop immigration but to defend the security of the nation and provide for law-and-order-based immigration. If we didn't defend our southern border then we would be saying that what God has so clearly stated to be important to Him was no longer important to our nation.

None of that stopped the anti-border people from speaking out vehemently against what they were once for, which used to include our established immigration laws. Indeed, the Democrat view of it morphed into a resistance to the Administration of President Trump despite the fact that the bipartisan concerns that encouraged the legislation to be initiated were still at our doorstep, only worse. The resistance delayed the implementation of building the Wall but eventually construction got underway and the administration negotiated policies with Mexico and the northern triangle countries of Central America that all but stopped what had been a near-crisis flow of illegal migration.

Nevertheless, highlighting an almost unbelievable lack of wisdom coupled with widespread voter fraud and Republican lack of foresight, we elected people to lead us in 2020 who value their politics more than the security of our nation and its people. Democrats who once supported the idea of a WALL are now opposed and Republicans couldn't get it finished even when they were in power. Wall construction stopped in 2021 and the gates have been opened to allow hundreds of thousands of illegal migrants into our country. God's borders are scarcely visible.

Disregard for Established Law

The Bible says that the End Times will be characterized by lawlessness.[75] And another thing you may not be aware of is that there's current immigration law in place that calls for an annual limit of 675,000 new immigrants plus specific allowances for accompanying family members.[76] The application of that law results in about one million immigrants per year who go through the established legal process. There are more than that number that enter illegally as undocumented aliens. Government data tries to convince us that the undocumented alien situation isn't that great, that it has been declining since the beginning of the Obama Administration. But they are not telling us the updated truth. Data is being manipulated, statistical methodology lacks consistency and the 11 million undocumented aliens they claim are presently living in our country is more like perhaps 25-30 million which can be reasonably assumed by making a couple of common-sense extrapolations. Let me emphasize that the people who are living in this country and have bypassed the established immigration laws are here illegally. Also, according to the dictionary, it is correct to call someone who is living here illegally an ALIEN accurately defined as:

A foreigner, especially one who is not a naturalized citizen of the country where they are living and still a subject or citizen of a foreign country.[77]

Our immigration laws are not immoral in any biblical sense and ought to be enforced. If our local, state and/or federal officials ignore the established legislation, they are part of the problem of lawlessness. If we will not regulate immigration into our country, then we have no border and we cease to be a nation that God can use as a base for the Great Commission. So, Christians who have become part of the resistance are also resisting Scripture. As previously discussed, the Bible doesn't require us to open our borders, it does *not* require us to take care of unlimited numbers of unhappy, even needy aliens and it does *not* require us to accommodate anyone who is here illegally. In fact, it's the contrary because Scripture DOES require the aliens among us to be subject to our laws.

In sum, since national borders are set by God, Christian believers are required to be good stewards over how we protected and defended God's boundaries. We need to pass and observe laws that provide security but allow for responsible administration. God has blessed America which is why we are exceptional in the world and why so many people want to come here. Almost everyone who wants to would become better off economically after they immigrate here. But for our own good, we're not able to assimilate more than some reasonable number which will always be a subjective determination. Yes, strategically located barrier walls are expensive but the related cost represents a minor inconvenience compared to the cost of supporting millions of undocumented aliens and the economic collapse of our country.

There are politicians in both major political parties who say now that border walls are not necessary, that it would be an unnecessary use of funds. Yet, many of them held the opposite position just a few years ago before the current administration (Biden-Harris) took office. Experts in the field almost unanimously agree that strategically located walls would be a powerful means for impeding the entry of undocumented aliens. Which group has the most credibility: the politicians who change their values based on political strategy, or immigration experts who are charged with the responsibility of enforcing our official immigration laws? Similarly, are we to believe our politicians whose values are like dust or the testimony of other countries who already have walls and, with no reason for lying, tell us they have been effective deterrents? Meanwhile as this update is being written, our southern border is contending with an illegal migrant invasion that has reached crisis proportions while Washington DC twiddles.

The Bible and Walls

Before leaving this chapter there are several interesting things the Bible has to say about walls. For one thing, there are walls all over it including Jerusalem, the city that Jesus wept for. And before you jump to the wrong conclusion that those walls were only for folks a long time ago, the Bible says that someday there will be a substantial wall around the future New Jerusalem.[78] In sum, there is a wall still in the future designed and set in place by God Almighty. What you may or may not know depending on how much you've studied your Bible is that the New Jerusalem wall will be there after God has permanently dealt with all the lawless people on the planet who have refused to accept His Son and submit to His ways of doing things. That last wall will not be for security. It won't be for safety. Rather, it will be there to remind Christian believers living within that God is their Source and Protector.

"God help us with more wisdom and truthfulness for our leaders! Convict them to govern according to your wishes in order to protect us from the world's evil. And let them know somehow that the future for ALL liars is perilous.[79] Thank you Father."

"Bless, O Lord, all the people of this land, from the highest to the lowest, particularly those whom Thou has appointed to rule us in church & state.

Excerpted from the personal Prayer Book of
President George Washington,
Written in his own hand

Eleven:

Prophetic Dedications

Secular people try really hard to exclude God from our exceptional country but He just goes ahead with whatever He wants to do so that truth can prevail. They try to either revise the truth or discredit it or rearrange it which is actually a futile exercise considering that truth is absolute and immutable. Nevertheless, they try to substitute counterfeit "truth" that most people somehow sense doesn't seem quite right. I have been amused when such "intelligent" and worldly-wise people care so much about the truth that they do and say whatever they have to trying to overcome it.

It has not always been this way in America. In the beginning the people of God spoke the truth out of their faith and proclaimed a great and enviable future for their new country. Contrary to secular attempts to revise history, almost all of the early leaders of America were seasoned bible-believing

Christians who lived by faith. Thus, we started out as a Christian nation, not a theocracy but a republic that operated openly on the basis of biblical values and principles. Some of those leaders spoke prophetically and went so far as to dedicate the U.S. to God which had never been done before. The words spoken by leaders of countries are often accompanied by a supernatural power of fulfillment and this has been a special aspect of the development of America into an exceptional country. In this chapter you will find two of the most relevant dedications in our history that most people don't know about.

The Prophetic Dedication of Pastor Robert Hunt[80]

The first permanent European colony in America was the Jamestown colony on the east coast of Virginia. It was started in 1607 and thrived for nearly 100 years as the capital of the Virginia colony. It was eventually abandoned when the capital was moved to Williamsburg in 1699.

The 105 colonists and seamen who set sail from England and settled at Jamestown carried *The Geneva Bible* with them. Those who studied its notes saw it as their mission to take the gospel to unknown lands and unsaved peoples. Before finding what would be their permanent settlement, Rev. Robert Hunt (1568–1608) offered the following prophetic prayer on April 29, 1607 at Cape Henry (now Virginia Beach, Virginia).

"We do hereby dedicate this Land, and ourselves, to reach the People within these shores with the Gospel of Jesus Christ, and to raise up Godly generations after us, and with these generations take the Kingdom of God to all the earth. May this Covenant of Dedication remain to all generations, as long as this earth remains, and may this Land, along with England, be Evangelist to the World. May all who see this Cross, remember what we have done here, and may those who come here to inhabit join us in this Covenant and in this most noble work that the Holy Scriptures may be fulfilled.

Using prophetic language, Hunt declared:

"*…from these very shores the Gospel shall go forth not only to this New World but the entire world.*"

The following Bible passage was read at the conclusion of the prayer:

"All the ends of the world shall remember and turn to the Lord, and all the kindreds of the nations shall worship before thee. For the kingdom is the Lord's and he ruleth among the nations."[81]

The Jamestown settlers believed in a covenantal approach to history whereby future generations would *"take the Kingdom of God to all the earth"*—and this is the key part—*"as long as this earth remains."* And importantly, these concepts came directly from the notes of *The Geneva Bible* with its kingdom-advancing vision just a few years before the publishing of *The King James Bible* in 1611.

The Geneva Bible provided much of the genius and inspiration that carried those courageous and faithful souls through their trials, and provided the spiritual, intellectual and legal basis for the success of the colonies. Thus, it became the foundation for the establishment of the American Nation and with it a legacy of individual Christian freedom for its people. God has set borders to protect this legacy for a people that have been prophetically set apart.

The Prophetic Dedication of George Washington

Another example of prophetic Christian leadership for America is our first president, George Washington. Thanks to secular historians there has been a never-ending discussion over what George Washington actually said in his inaugural address on April 30, 1789 and whether he was really a committed Christian or just some other kind of religious person.

There are at least three problems secular historians encounter when they try to reinterpret historical Christian truth from the 18th century. The first is that they have no real understanding of how Christianity works so their representations of it bear the errors of their ignorance. Secondly, they go into it with a bias that refuses to acknowledge the clear evidence that almost all of our founding fathers were bible-believing Christians which results in demonstrably wrong conclusions. And thirdly, the manner of their speaking back then is hard to understand especially if you aren't grounded in the related subject.

Here's the situation: when George Washington was inaugurated as our first President, he made a speech in New York City. In it, he clearly connected his new country to God but secular historians stubbornly refuse to see it that way. They persist in saying it had to have been some secular thing he said because George Washington wasn't a true Christian believer defying the clear historical evidence to the contrary. Following are two selected excerpts from what he actually said about God during the speech followed by my "translation" to modern English. A transcript or the entire speech can be found in Appendix A of this book. You be the judge:

What he said:
"It would be peculiarly improper to omit in this first official act my fervent supplications to that Almighty Being who rules over the universe, who presides in the councils of nations, and whose providential aids can supply every human defect, that His benediction may consecrate to the liberties and happiness of the people of the United States a Government instituted by themselves for these essential purposes.

"No people can be found to acknowledge and adore the Invisible Hand which conducts the affairs of men more than those of the United States. Every step by which they have advanced to the character of an inde-

pendent nation seems to have been distinguished by some token of providential agency…"[82]

My Modern Translation:
In my first official act it would be improper of me to neglect asking the almighty Ruler of the Universe, who presides over all nations of the earth and whose power can cure every human defect, to bless this new government with a lasting dedication to the purposes that the people have themselves instituted which are freedom and happiness for all.

No people on the earth love God more than the people of the United States. Indeed, every step they have taken in the creation of this new independent nation seems to have been a result of a providential plan of God.

Is it not obvious from these selected excerpts (for a true Christian) that President George Washington acknowledged that the creation of the United States of America was part of a providential plan of God? Is it not also obvious that the new President asked God to empower (bless) the new government with a continuing dedication to the fulfillment of the specific purposes the people had derived for themselves under that providential plan? If these things are true, then America is the only democratic country in the history of the world whose primary leader dedicated it to the plans and purposes of Creator God. It is our connection to God that has made us an exceptional country and the launch place for the Great Commission to disciple the nations.

In case you still aren't convinced about the Christianity of George Washington, I rejoice in the fact that I can provide irrefutable evidence with the following single entry among many in his private Prayer Journal:

Monday Morning:
"Direct my thoughts, words and work. Wash away my sins in the immaculate blood of the lamb, and purge my heart by thy Holy Spirit, from the dross of my natural corruption, that I may with more freedom of mind and liberty of will serve thee, the everlasting God, in righteousness and holiness this day, and all the days of my life.

"Increase my faith in the sweet promises of the Gospel. Give me repentance from dead works. Pardon my wanderings, & direct my thoughts unto thyself, the God of my salvation. Teach me how to live in thy fear, labor in thy service, and ever to run in the ways of thy commandments. Make me always watchful over my heart, that neither the terrors of conscience, the loathing of holy duties, the love of sin, nor an unwillingness to depart this life, may cast me into a spiritual slumber. But daily frame me more and more into the likeness of thy son Jesus Christ, that living in thy fear, and dying in thy favor, I may in thy appointed time attain the resurrection of the just unto eternal

life. Bless my family, friends & kindred unite us all in praising & glorifying thee in all our works begun, continued, and ended, when we shall come to make our last account before thee blessed Saviour, who hath taught us thus to pray, our Father."[83]

If you can't see the Christianity in this writing, please be sure to read Chapter 13 in this book. It will help you and you need it desperately.

• • •

If indeed the creation of the United States of America was part of God's providential plan and has been dedicated by its leaders to God's plans and purposes, then its borders have been set by Him like no other country in history. Tamper with our borders at your own risk! God has a purpose for this country to take the Gospel of Jesus Christ to the nations and His program relies on established borders. His plan will be carried out exactly as He wants it to be. God will build His Kingdom and the gates of hell shall not prevail against it![84]

"But the wisdom from above is first pure, then peaceable, gentle, reasonable, full of mercy and good fruits, unwavering, without hypocrisy."

James 3:17
New American Standard

Twelve

Aspiring to Christian Correctness

This chapter is perhaps the most important part of this book because it has to do with how true believers should be conducting themselves in the face of contentious issues like *opening our borders and unrestricted alien migration*. The first thing to keep in mind is that nothing about this subject has caught God by surprise. As a matter of fact, it was Jesus who said two thousand years ago that it is His Word that separates us from the world and makes them hate us.[85] He already knew this would be happening because God knows all things[86] and has taken them into account in establishing His plans and purposes.

Second, we should always consider the interests of the Kingdom of God as our highest priority as we deal with these issues. What does that mean? One thing it does NOT mean is that it's our job to establish His Kingdom in our own strength.

Establishing the Kingdom is mostly God's job. Ours is to focus on taking the gospel to the nations and being godly ambassadors to the world.[87] It is also not our job to *worry* about the politics of the day, or about the way people in the world are handling themselves, or about the status of particular issues in the midst of the confrontation. We are not to be anxious or overly emotional about these things keeping in mind that soon enough Jesus will be returning to put the finishing touches on His Kingdom no matter what happens on this planet about our little cultural confrontations.

But it *does* mean that as we make our decisions and pursue our strategies, we should consider how to best serve the interests of the Kingdom of God. How can true Christians support a candidate running on a platform that includes values that grossly disagree with the Bible? Personal agendas are always to be a lower priority than the interests of His Kingdom and too often this is a problem for "believers."

We ought to avoid getting *overly* wrapped up in the *politics* of these issues realizing that the confrontation taking place is actually a spiritual matter. The world makes it political but we should know better. We may more closely identify with one of the political parties and its agenda, but none of that is as important as the Kingdom of God. We can enter into spiritual warfare against the Adversary but yelling and screeching and speaking disrespectfully to or about people among the opposition isn't a righteous strategy for God's people. I think believers are being really challenged these days to control their emotions and passions and their ways of speaking so we're able to refrain from operating in the flesh like the unavoidable default position of the other side.

Notice I'm saying we should not be *"overly"* wrapped up in politics specifically related to our emotions and anxieties. This doesn't mean believers should avoid running for political office. In fact, we need MORE righteous Christians running for political office than ever before, including clergy. Ignoring politics isn't the answer. That strategy has proven to be ineffective. We *should* be involved in the political process emphasizing the values of the Kingdom and not allowing ourselves to operate the way the world does as we're seeking political office.

Another thing to take into account is that the Bible says we're to *love* our neighbors.[88] Not only that, we're also supposed to love our enemies:

"…I tell you, love your enemies and pray for those who persecute you…"[89]

We love God first and other people second. To be clear about this, the meaning of the original Greek Bible word *agape,* translated as *love* in these scriptures and as discussed previously, is a special unconditional, self-sacrificing kind of love. It rises above the particular political agendas arrayed against us, above what their rhetoric sounds like, or what their *political* beliefs are. We are to love them anyway and mourn for their unbelief that presently condemns them to an eternity separated from God. We defend the Kingdom because of our love for God. We take the gospel to the world because we love its people too, even though they hate us.

Most people who want to immigrate to America want to have a better life for themselves. Who can blame them? As Christians we love all people. We're not about *closed borders*. That's a false representation of bible-based arguments against *open borders*. We're right to depict *open borders* as a dumb, wisdom-challenged idea that happens to also be unbiblical and counter to the expressed will of God. But we should advocate with *open arms* for rational immigration, just not with *open borders*. In other words, we should be advocating for *regulated borders* that protect the people who already live here but provide lawful and orderly opportunities to people who want to come here, work hard and live according to our laws in harmony with our prevailing culture.

There are at least three basic groups of *neighbors* in the world who want to come here:

- Those seeking God's freedom.
- Those seeking God's medical healing.
- Those seeking God's economic prosperity.

Should we not advocate for a system of laws and procedures that provide orderly immigration and work-related visas? Should we not demand that our elected officials in Congress overcome their political paralysis and make this happen? What is more important: The Kingdom of God or the agendas of the political parties they represent?

There are, of course, other people who want to come here to engage in illegal enterprise or to foment political unrest. We don't need them here and it is a really naïve idea to consider letting them come here, especially the ones who openly want to kill us. But the others, the people who can contribute and want to work and to be Americans realizing that we are fundamentally an English-speaking country founded on Judeo-Christian bible values and free enterprise, the ones who aren't just looking for government handouts, we can indeed let those come among us in a lawful, orderly, wise and measured way.

As we come to the end of this book, I also want to make the point that according to Scripture, the wisdom of God that's so needed for the *open borders* debate comes with certain characteristics. Scripture says His wisdom is pure, peaceable, gentle, reasonable, filled with both mercy and good fruits, unwavering and without hypocrisy.[90] Unbelievers don't have access to this kind of wisdom so their ideas often don't make sense. But they can't help being that way because their minds have been blinded by the Adversary to the wisdom and benefits of God.[91]

We who *do* know God, who *do* have access to His wisdom, must keep in mind that the access comes by the Spirit and not by the flesh. If we allow ourselves to get all angry and frustrated and animated and emotional and worried over this issue or when confronted by the arguments of the world, then we won't be walking in the Spirit. We will be in the flesh and our arguments won't take us where we want to be.

It's God's job to make His Word work. It's His anointing that breaks the yokes that bind.[92] All we can do is stay in love, make His biblical principles known to those we're contending with and then let Him do the heavy lifting. Hateful speech gains nothing. Failing to control our speaking produces nothing of value for the Kingdom. If we tell the truth with sincere love behind it, our points of view will prevail because God can always work with truth and love. It definitely *is* our job to speak out the truth knowing that the world will hate both the message and the messenger. If they don't hear the truth from us, who will tell them?

I'm also compelled to mention here that our Pastors need to speak out more fearlessly and more forcefully from their pulpits about PC in general and *open borders* in particular. Many Pastors today are of the mindset that they should not speak at all about *politics*. It is indeed a good thing we had different thinking among a patriot clergy in Revolutionary War times because according to the British generals and their King, the American clergy was the reason the British lost their colony.[93] They blamed their loss on the active involvement of the American clergy in explaining the biblical basis for the Revolution to their congregations, in the recruiting of soldiers and in the armed confrontations on the battlefield.

This is what many of our Pastors today are missing: this isn't about politics. It's about the Kingdom of God. It's about staying free to take the gospel to the nations all over the earth. And it's about conducting spiritual warfare against the Adversary. The confrontation isn't about politics, it's about truth and the Word of God. The world says it's about politics and when our Pastors agree with them, they put themselves on the wrong track. When they say that Christian activists don't speak in love, they put themselves in agreement with the world and they *judge* well-meaning, bible-believing Christians as lacking in love even though no one sees their hearts.

Jesus loved the Pharisees when to their faces he called them *vipers.* That was some severe name calling that today's silent Christians would have been quick to judge! Jesus loved them as well when He cleansed the Temple behind a whip He had fashioned with His own hands.[94] How is it then that current-day activists who have the love of God abiding in us are frequently judged negatively by so many Christians, who have otherwise chosen to remain silent, for the particular words we choose in speaking out the truth? It's not all that easy anyway to separate love from truth for they are both the essence of Christ. Do the silent Christians truly love their neighbors if they are unwilling to enter fully into the battle for the winning of their souls?

The bottom line is that shepherds are supposed to lead and the sheep will follow. Today the sheep are confused. On the whole, they tend not to vote at election time, they shy away from the work that's necessary to deal with today's secular environment, they don't want to run for political office and they mostly complain and stay home milling around in their little circles waiting for their shepherds to show up. We need leadership NOW to re-invigorate the Body of Christ! Perhaps if we were more proficient at following our orders and implementing the Great Commission, there would be fewer people having to try to come into our country illegally to receive what God has for them.

Summary

Finally, I haven't said anywhere that these things would be easy. But by the Holy Spirit, they are at least possible. In fact, with God, *ALL* things are possible.[95] We don't have to be perfect; we just have to try the best we can and God will work with it. Here is a summary based on Scripture of the major things I believe the Church should be standing for in regard to the subject of our borders:

1. Christians should stand against both open and closed borders. Rather, we should advocate for *managed* borders that are clearly defined and energetically defended.

2. Christians should stand against all forms of socialism because it's a system that is based in *covetousness* and naturally usurps the freedom that comes from God.

3. Christians should always protect and support the agenda and priorities of the Kingdom of God over their own agendas and the priorities of men.

4. Christians should always stand for biblical correctness when it is contradicted by political correctness.

5. Christians should always stand against lawlessness and the subversion of truth.

6. Christians should not be so eager to publicly accuse, condemn and criticize other Christians for how they choose to deal with these issues. It's okay to be vocal in support for the things of God but not okay to be accusing and criticizing each other publicly. It is just as bad to criticize a fellow believer for not being active and vocal enough as it is to accuse one of us for not being loving enough in the way they pursue their assignments. Who are we to judge the servant of another?[96]

7. When we are vocal and forthright in our stances, we should strive to bring the truth in love by avoiding anger and choosing softer words than our flesh usually wants us to use.

8. Christians should vote in EVERY election. God has given us the blessing of participating with Him in the choosing of our elected officials. It is a delegated portion of God's authority to set our leaders in place[97] and we are one of the few countries in the history of the world to have received such authority. Along with that comes the responsibility of exercising our delegated authority. It is a matter of stewarding something that belongs to God. <u>To not vote is to disrespect the authority of God</u>. And of course, we want to be informed so we can vote for candidates that we know will protect and benefit the Kingdom of God, not according to political parties and not according to our personal agendas.

   Did you know that almost half of all professing Christians are not registered to vote? If you are 18 years of age, a U.S. citizen and meet your state's residency requirements, you ought to be registered and then vote in every election. Many states don't allow convicted felons to vote. Undocumented aliens who are in our country illegally should not be allowed to vote.

9. Christians should be making every effort to find ways for the Body of Christ to unite. However, I

> know that many Christians will jump to disagree with the message of this book even though I have shown you an abundance of Scripture to back up everything I have written. Consequently, your argument will be with the Word instead of me.
>
> As I have written this book, I have studied various other points of view I hadn't considered before which has helped me acquire a broader vision. Now I ask those who might disagree with this message to at least reconsider their positions so that we can find a way to unite ourselves together for the purpose of performing the true will of God. None of us has all the answers and instead of allowing that to divide us, we should rather be looking for the whole truth that will bring us all together in the sincere pursuit of God's plan and purpose for the nations.

In the meantime, we can be praying that Congress will finally pass godly, bible-based legislation that will shut down the socialist idea of *open borders* once and for all so we can continue to be a country that celebrates individual freedom and provides a base from which the Gospel, the too good to be true news from the Kingdom of God, can go forth to the nations. Pray also for the building of the wall!

Following is a bumper sticker a dear friend sent me just as I was finishing the original version of this book. It explains a lot and is followed by a special view of these things as seen by a local artist friend.

HEAVEN

HAS A WALL AND STRICT
IMMIGRATION POLICIES

HELL

HAS OPEN BORDERS

The Truth About Open Borders

Dr. Bill Miller

If you confess with your mouth Jesus as Lord,
and believe in your heart that God raised
Him from the dead, you will be saved...

Romans 10:9
American Standard Bible

Thirteen:

Are You a Christian Believer?

As discussed in this book, the Creator God of the universe has established the borders and boundaries of all nations. We tend to think we're the ones who did it and that we can move them around however we want to, or disrespect them if we want to. Or ignore them as we choose to. It is our nature to resist God.

To make a long story short, that nature of ours got us into trouble with Him a long time ago and eventually He had to send His Son Jesus to make amends and give us a way to reconcile things. An arrangement was made for that to happen but we each have to decide if we want to be involved in the arrangement. It's our decision to make one way or the other.

God revealed the details of all this in His Bible. That's the same Bible we talked about in the early chapters that's been causing all the commotion. You see, most people are rejecting the idea of being a part of the arrangement that Jesus worked out for us and they resent the idea that the Bible insists so adamantly that they're all making the wrong decision. They don't want there to be negative consequences to what they've decided to do in their lives.

All of us start out in life pre-programmed to resist God and His Bible. That's contrary to what many folks have been taught, but it's what the Bible actually says. We're not born as innocent babes and it's that sin nature we ARE born with that separates us from God and made it necessary for Jesus to come and work out something for us. Fortunately, we don't have to DO anything to get involved in His arrangement except make a few decisions:

- ✓ Decide that we no longer want to be controlled by our sin nature. The Bible calls that repentance.
- ✓ Decide that God exists and wants to help us.
- ✓ Decide to accept the authority of Jesus over our lives and speak out about it.
- ✓ Decide to believe in our hearts that God raised Jesus from the dead on our behalf.

Now there are two groups of people this chapter is intended for: those who have never thought of themselves as Christian believers and others who have called themselves Christians but have never allowed Jesus to be their Lord. He wants to be both Savior and Lord but He can't be Savior unless you also make Him Lord.

You now know from reading this book that what the Bible actually says about the subject of borders and boundaries is largely different than what you hear in our culture. And, there are a lot of other subjects that fit that same description including what it takes to be a true Christian.

If you are now motivated to align yourself with the Truth by making Jesus your Lord, or if you want to reconfirm that He is your Lord, you can speak the following declaration out loud believing what you say with all your heart:

Jesus, I declare today with all my heart that I believe in you and I believe that God raised you from the dead. I acknowledge that my sins have been forgiven for all time and I ask you to come into my life today and be my Lord and Savior. I receive your forgiveness and thank you for salvation and eternal life.

If you were sincere as you spoke out these words, God has already come into your life and you're a new creation, a new person recreated in His image. It's important to go now and tell someone what has happened to you. Then ask the Lord to lead you to a good faith-based, bible-teaching church where you can be equipped to fulfill your potential in the Kingdom of God.

When you get a moment, have someone help you look up the following scriptures because they confirm what you've done by saying this prayer and believing what you said:

Romans 10:9

2 Corinthians 5:17

Ephesians 2:8

Receive the Baptism of the Holy Spirit

Once you become a child of God, your loving heavenly Father wants to give you a supernatural empowerment so that you can live the exciting new life He has in mind for you. According to the Bible, all you have to do is ask Him for it and then believe that you receive it the same way you believed that you received salvation and eternal life when you simply asked Him for them.

Just pray the following way and believe: *Father God, I recognize my need for Your power to live this new life the way You want me to. I acknowledge that when I was born again, I received your Holy Spirit to dwell in me and I ask you for the full release of His power which I now receive as an act of faith according to the promise in Your Word.*

That's all it takes to receive the fullness of God's super-natural power and now that it has come upon you, some syllables from a language you don't recognize will begin to rise up from your inner person and into your mouth (1 Corinthians 14:14). As you speak them out loud by faith, you'll be releasing God's power from within and it will strengthen you (1 Corinthians 14:4).

The Bible calls this *"Speaking in Tongues"* and you can do this whenever and wherever you choose. When you speak this way, direct it to God in the form of a prayer and even though you may not understand what you are saying, God WILL understand because it will be the Holy Spirit within you giving the utterances you're speaking.

You can also ask Him for the related interpretation which you can receive by faith just like any other communication from God. Test it against the Word and your inner witness and if it passes the test, run with it by faith.

May God now bless you with hunger for His Word and the revelation of who He is!

So, What Did You Think of the Book?

First of all, thanks for purchasing it. I know you could have picked any number of books to read, but you picked this one and I'm really grateful.

I hope it added value to your life and helped you develop a more complete biblical perspective. If so, it would be really helpful if you would please share this book with your friends and family by posting your positive comments on Facebook, Twitter and other social media. We really appreciate your help!

Also, if you enjoyed the book and believe the message needs to get out to as many people as possible, please take a few moments to post a review on Amazon. Just go to this link:

https://www.amazon.com/gp/product/1725799065/ref=dbs_a_def_rwt_bibl_vppi_i1

I want you to know that your review is very important for the Body of Christ. It will raise our rankings with Amazon which will make it possible for more people to see it and find out what the Bible actually says about our borders.

If you aren't sure how to make a review, the next page goes into a little more detail. Come and be a part of this important ministry. May God especially bless you for making this extra effort!

How to Write and Submit a Review

Writing a review on Amazon is really easy. Just go to the book's front page and under the heading Customer Reviews, you will see a button for writing a review. Click on it and you will be taken to a page set up for 'Your Reviews' where you can write reviews for your purchases.

What you do is:

1. Select the **rating** of the book from 1-5 stars, with 5 being the best score.

2. Write your **book description** in the box provided. Keep in mind that if you leave this page before submitting your review, you'll have to start over again. I would recommend writing the review first in Word or Evernote and then copy and paste.

3. **Create a headline** for the review.

4. Hit **submit**. Your review will go live within a couple of hours, although it could take up to 24 hours.

One point to be clear about here is that according to Amazon's policy for posting reviews, you have to have an account that has **made a purchase of at least $50** using a valid credit or debit card.

Appendix A:

GEORGE WASHINGTON'S INAUGURAL ADDRESS[98]

April 30, 1789

Fellow Citizens of the Senate and the House of Representatives.

Among the vicissitudes incident to life, no event could have filled me with greater anxieties than that of which the notification was transmitted by your order, and received on the fourteenth day of the present month. On the one hand, I was summoned by my Country, whose voice I can never hear but with veneration and love, from a retreat which I had chosen with the fondest predilection, and, in my flattering hopes, with an immutable decision, as the asylum of my declining years: a retreat which was rendered every day more necessary as well as more dear to me, by the addition of habit to inclination, and of frequent interruptions in my health to the gradual waste committed on it by time. On the other hand, the magnitude and difficulty of the trust to which the voice of my Country called me, being sufficient to awaken in the wisest and most experienced of her citizens, a distrustful scrutiny into his qualifications, could not but overwhelm with dispondence, one, who, inheriting inferior endowments from nature and unpractised in the duties of civil administration, ought to be peculiarly conscious of his own deficiencies. In this conflict of emotions, all I dare aver, is, that it has been my faithful study to collect my duty from a just appreciation of every circumstance, by which it might be affected. All I dare hope, is, that, if in executing this task I have been too much swayed by a grateful remembrance of former instances, or by an affectionate sensibility to this transcendent proof, of the confidence of my fellow-citizens; and have thence too little consulted my incapacity as well as disinclination for the weighty and untried cares before me; my error will be palliated by the motives which misled me, and its consequences be judged by my Country, with some share of the partiality in which they originated.

Such being the impressions under which I have, in obedience to the public summons, repaired to the present station; it would be peculiarly improper to omit in this first official Act, my fervent supplications to that Almighty Being who rules over the Universe, who presides in the Councils of Nations, and whose providential aids can supply every human defect, that his benediction may consecrate to the liberties and happiness of the People of the United States, a Government instituted by themselves for these essential purposes: and may enable every instrument employed in its administration to execute with success, the functions allotted to his charge. In tendering this homage to the Great Author of every public and private good I assure myself that it expresses your sentiments not less than my own; nor those of my fellow-citizens at large, less than either. No People can be bound to acknowledge and adore the invisible hand, which conducts the Affairs of men more than the People of the United States. Every step, by which they have advanced to the character of an independent nation, seems to have been distinguished by some token of providential agency. And in the important revolution just accomplished in the system of their United Government, the tranquil deliberations and voluntary consent of so many distinct communities, from which the event has resulted, cannot be compared with the means by which most Governments have been established, without some return of pious gratitude along with an humble anticipation of the future blessings which the past seem to presage. These reflections, arising out of the present crisis, have forced themselves too strongly on my mind to be suppressed. You will join with me I trust in thinking, that there are none under the influence of which, the proceedings of a new and free Government can more auspiciously commence.

By the article establishing the Executive Department, it is made the duty of the President "to recommend to your consideration, such measures as he shall judge necessary and expedient." The circumstances under which I now meet you, will acquit me from entering into that subject, farther than to refer to the Great Constitutional Charter under which you are assembled; and which, in defining your powers, designates the objects to which your attention is to be given. It will be more consistent with those circumstances, and far more congenial with the feelings which actuate me, to substitute, in place of a recommendation of particular measures, the tribute that is due to the talents, the rectitude, and the patriotism which adorn the characters selected to devise and adopt them. In these honorable qualifications, I behold the surest pledges, that as on one side, no local prejudices, or attachments; no seperate views, nor party animosities, will misdirect the comprehensive and equal eye which ought to watch over this great assemblage of communities and interests: so, on another, that the foundations of our National policy will be laid in the pure and immutable principles of private morality; and the pre-eminence of a free Government, be exemplified by all the attributes which can win the affections of its Citizens, and command the respect of the world.

I dwell on this prospect with every satisfaction which an ardent love for my Country can inspire: since there is no truth more thoroughly established, than that there exists in the economy and course of nature, an indissoluble union between virtue and happiness, between duty and advantage, between the genuine maxims of an honest and magnanimous policy, and the solid rewards of public prosperity and felicity: Since we ought to be no less persuaded that the propitious smiles of Heaven, can never be expected on a nation that disregards the eternal rules of order and right, which Heaven itself has ordained: And since the preservation of the sacred fire of liberty, and the destiny of the Republican model of Government, are justly considered as deeply, perhaps as finally staked, on the experiment entrusted to the hands of the American people.

Besides the ordinary objects submitted to your care, it will remain with your judgment to decide, how far an exercise of the occasional power delegated by the Fifth article of the Constitution is rendered expedient at the present juncture by the nature of objections which have been urged against the System, or by the degree of inquietude which has given birth to them. Instead of undertaking particular recommendations on this subject, in which I could be guided by no lights derived from official opportunities, I shall again give way to my entire confidence in your discernment and pursuit of the public good: For I assure myself that whilst you carefully avoid every alteration which might endanger the benefits of an United and effective Government, or which ought to await the future lessons of experience; a reverence for the characteristic rights of freemen, and a regard for the public harmony, will sufficiently influence your deliberations on the question how far the former can be more impregnably fortified, or the latter be safely and advantageously promoted.

To the preceeding observations I have one to add, which will be most properly addressed to the House of Representatives. It concerns myself, and will therefore be as brief as possible. When I was first honoured with a call into the Service of my Country, then on the eve of an arduous struggle for its liberties, the light in which I contemplated my duty required that I should renounce every pecuniary compensation. From this resolution I have in no instance departed. And being still under the impressions which produced it, I must decline as inapplicable to myself, any share in the personal emoluments, which may be indispensably included in a permanent provision for the Executive Department; and must accordingly pray that the pecuniary estimates for the Station in which I am placed, may, during my continuance in it, be limited to such actual expenditures as the public good may be thought to require.

Having thus imparted to you my sentiments, as they have been awakened by the occasion which brings us together, I shall take my present leave; but not without resorting once more to the benign parent of the human race, in humble supplication that since he has been pleased to favour the American people, with opportunities for deliberating in perfect tranquility, and dispositions for deciding with unparellelled unanimity on a form of Government, for the security of their Union, and the advancement of their happiness; so his divine blessing may be equally *conspicuous* in the enlarged views, the temperate consultations, and the wise measures on which the success of this Government must depend.

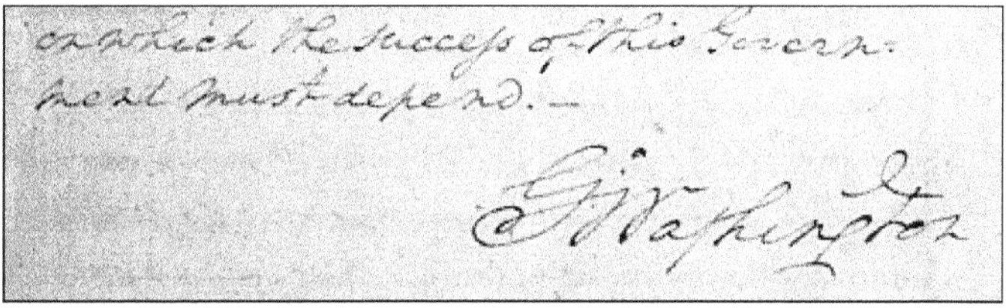
on which the success of this Govern-
ment must depend.—
G° Washington

Washington's distinctive signature

Appendix B:

Border Security and the U.S. Pastor Council

Back in 2010, the US Pastor Council (USPC) headquartered in Houston, Texas observed that many Pastors in their area were having to deal with tension and fear among their growing Spanish-speaking memberships. The tension stemmed from immigration uncertainty caused by the broken immigration system coupled with an intensification of politically conservative rhetoric being aimed at the growing undocu-mented alien situation. So, the USPC decided to put a position paper together that would help pastors deal with the immigrant situation by clarifying and standing on biblical truth.

The following Declaration was released in 2010 and it challenges our leaders to fix the immigration system once and for all so that uncertainty can be eliminated. Additionally, with their pastors behind them, the immigrants who were already here were able to acquire a certain level of peace. Pastors taught the TRUTH about immigration which also comforted. Such were the results that the idea was carried to other states and to date more than 1500 pastors in 22 states have signed this unique Declaration as of the publication of this book in late 2018.

One of the important conclusions to take away from this declaration is that the Church and its Pastor leaders cannot take a stance of passivity by avoiding the issue of illegal migration. Christians need the truth and if they don't receive it from their Pastors, they have no choice but to listen to the secular world who is not bashful about making its views known. God will hold us accountable for how we led the stewardship of His important boundaries and borders.

Pastors' Declaration on Border Security and Immigration Reform*

Preamble

In the course of our history as a nation, challenges and crisis moments have arisen that required principled leadership and the laying aside of partisan politics. Such is the need before us in our day regarding the escalating illegal immigration crisis and the security of our national borders.

It is clear and evident that the tangible and present crisis regarding the state of our national border security and immigration system must be addressed rapidly, justly and humanely with equal regard to both rule of law and God-given value of every individual. Holy Scriptures demand that justice and compassion be balanced with neither improperly dominant over the other in our hearts and our laws.

Therefore, we as pastoral leaders called by God to proclaim His truth and acting in the tradition of our nation's history to lift our voice in the public square when there are those societal issues that demand just action by our governing representatives, do hereby present this statement of general principles and call on our elected state and national leaders to:

- End the contentious political posturing and bickering that is polarizing our nation.

- Engage in genuine dialogue and come together to arrive at real solutions to this crisis.

- Listen to the voice of the majority of people who demand secure borders, credible enforcement of our current immigration laws by our federal government, reforming the broken immigration system, and humanely addressing those who have entered the country illegally.

- Recognize and acknowledge that this crisis would already be resolved if past administrations and Congresses had exercised courageous leadership and had been willing to work together to take the necessary steps for resolution.

- Pledge to resolve this crisis by taking courageous, decisive and immediate steps to deal with and implement the following call to action.

We call on every member of the Texas State Legislature and the United States Congress to publicly support and provide proactive leadership to see this present crisis resolved in a humane way that includes but is not limited to the following steps IN THIS ORDER of priority:

Step One – Secure our National Borders First

It is the first business of our government to protect the safety and welfare of citizens against "enemies foreign and domestic." The well- established fact that drug cartels, gang members, other criminal elements and now Middle Eastern operatives linked to Islamic terrorism are freely moving across our southern border has created an urgent national security crisis.

ACTION NEEDED:

- All borders, with specific priority to the southern border of the United States, must be secured as soon as possible using whatever means necessary to stop all entry from points other than regulated crossing stations.

- Fences, adequately armed U.S. military presence, electronic surveillance, increased Border Patrol forces, full enforcement of all existing immigration laws and policy changes protecting citizens as well as law enforcement from persecution, prosecution or lawsuits when acting to protect life and property are examples of first steps that need to be implemented.

Step Two – Reform the Immigration System

The process of entering the country legally is fraught with red tape, fraud, delays, unacceptable costs, unrealistically low quotas and inhumane treatment for many if not most people who desire to emigrate to the U.S. temporarily for education or work, or permanently as citizens. This system needs to be reformed so people legitimately seeking temporary or permanent residency in this country are treated with dignity and respect.

ACTION NEEDED:

- Government agencies charged with assessing and processing immigration requests are severely understaffed and inadequately funded to handle the backlog of immigration applications. Current staffing at American embassies charged with assessing and processing immigration applications should be better trained, better screened and/or replaced as necessary with uniform standards provided for greater accountability.

- Congress needs to reform immigration laws to address significant backlogs under quotas for highly skilled immigrants; to establish meaningful quotas for semi and low -skilled workers as well as enact a temporary worker program so that where there are proven shortages of U. S. workers, there is a mechanism by which workers can enter legally while maintaining their family ties to their home countries. Congress also needs to modernize the verification process by which employers determine who is authorized to work in the U. S.

Step Three – Implement a just process to legal status for specified illegal immigrants

While illegal immigrants have violated immigration laws to enter the country or overstayed their lawfully permitted time, there needs to be a process of providing those who qualify, are involved in lawful commerce and wish to remain here a means of doing so either as guest workers or eventually as citizens, with the proviso that they be required to display proficiency in the English language and critical facts about our American history, the basis of our

Constitutional republic and the duties of citizenship within a reasonable period of time to qualify for either status.

ACTION NEEDED:

- ☐ Execute a fixed period of open registration for those here illegally, and provide a temporary work visa which contains requirement of adequate civil penalties yet does not require them to return to their country of origin and provides protection of legal status. Once that registration period has passed, any violation of immigration laws should result in immediate deportation.

- ☐ Any person found to have committed crimes against property or person while here, or with a felony criminal record in his or her home country, should be denied legal status of any kind and deported.

- ☐ Effectively enforce laws which prohibit non-citizens from receiving entitlement to nonemergency government services unless specifically adopted by legislative process at the state or federal level.

We the undersigned pastors declare our commitment to using our voice and influence in every way possible to support these principles. We will also publicly hold accountable those who choose to remain silent, who are divisive for purely political purposes, or who act in opposition to these principles.

** Created by the U.S. Pastor Council and signed in 2010*

The foregoing Pastors' Declaration has been signed by more than 1,500 Pastors and Ministers in 22 states. You can contact the principals of the U.S. Pastor Council as follows:

U.S. Pastor Council
P.O. Box 692207
Houston, TX 77269

832-688-9166 Phone
832-688-8484 Fax

www.uspastorcouncil.org

Appendix C:

The Truth about American Exceptionalism

Article by Dr. Bill Miller first published July 26, 2019:

I'm sure you've noticed lately that there are lots of people in our country who don't like it all that much and want to pretty much change everything. They tend to be associated with our universities and the Democrat Party, and they're really vocal about their dissatisfaction. But if you stop and think for a moment, what is the rationale behind condemning one's own country? What can be gained from that? Years ago, when I used to travel a lot, I visited MANY places that didn't have very much, but the people all loved their own countries even when there was oppression.

The obvious truth is that by almost any rational measure, the *United States of America* has been the most exceptional country that ever existed: economically, militarily, influentially and just about any way you look at it. That doesn't mean we've been perfect, but nothing that people put together is ever perfect. The unique thing about America though is that we try to bring correction to our imperfections, not by divisive complaining and condemnation but by trying to work together and then doing whatever we have to do to bring about majority-approved change.

One of the imperfections we've heard so much about in particular these days is the matter of slavery and no one can be proud of that part of our history. It was an abomination that started 257 years before America even became a country and it was eventually eradicated 80 years later after the loss of 700,000 lives in the Civil War. A new country faced a major inherited flaw, embarked on a sacrificially radical process to correct it and then somehow came back together as a country. Too bad that so many folks can't focus on the exceptional outcome instead of the flawed history that preceded it.

But that's only one of the issues anti-exceptional people bring up. There are many things they are unhappy about because there's actually a spiritual problem at the root of all their complaining. You see, America is exceptional because it was founded as a Christian nation and built on a foundation of Bible-based principles and values. I know that a lot of people don't want to acknowledge this aspect of our history, but the truth is the truth and it never changes even if people want it to and even if they try to revise it.

Here's the crux of it: people who are anti-God and anti-Bible attack the idea that America is exceptional because exceptionalism validates the influence of God in our history. Almost all of them believe they are arguing a political issue, but it's a spiritual issue and they are at odds with God and His Bible. It's His testimony to the world: our country has been exceptional as a consequence of our historical reliance on God. By attacking exceptionalism, they purpose to do damage to the idea of divine involvement in the affairs of America.

Unfortunately, most of the people who can't see American exceptionalism are also unable to see God, and that's the real tragedy. It's tragic because most of them are rejecting Jesus, the one person who could make them into exceptional people with exceptional futures. Nevertheless, instead of despising the folks who decry our exceptionalism, we're called to love them, to lovingly resist their agenda and to pray for the truth to get through to them before it's too late.

Appendix D:

Selected Articles about American Freedom

The articles in this section have appeared in newspapers and on line over a number of years usually in celebration of the fourth of July. They are also part of a free publication called *The Little Book of Freedom* that is available from the publisher of this book upon request. It is an E-book that you will enjoy.

In the meantime, these special articles are a good fit as supplemental reading in connection with the topics of borders and immigration. We are a free country and people want to come here. What isn't fully understood though is that true freedom comes from God and only from God. If you enjoy freedom, you must opt for the presence of God. To exclude God from the culture is to extinguish freedom and make *America the Beautiful* look like so many other countries that thought they were smarter than God.

Free people live within borders and are submitted to the rule of God-influenced laws and self-control.

1 - The Origin of Freedom

July is FREEDOM month in America and it's wonderful to live in a FREE country. But have you ever thought about where our freedom came from? The Bible says Freedom was God's idea and that Jesus came so all people could be free. Moreover, it says that knowing the TRUTH is what sets us free (John 8:32), that Jesus is the TRUTH (John 14:6) and that wherever His SPIRIT is present there's FREEDOM (2 Corinthians 3:17).

We tend to think of FREEDOM as a political thing. But governments and people by their nature will eventually work toward the control of society and the suppression of freedom. History confirms this and what it also confirms is that the ONLY way to avoid an ultimate destiny of bondage is by having God involved as much as possible in the process of ongoing governance. No friend, real freedom can ONLY come from the presence of God, not because I say so but because the Bible says it.

The folks who started our country must surely have been some of the wisest people who ever walked the planet. Many of them had grown up during the *First Great Awakening* (1730-1755) and had learned about true freedom from their Pastors. At the time though, they were living under an English monarchy that was progressively suppressing their freedom and they weren't all that happy about it. In other words, their rulers were operating in a way that contradicted their understanding of Scripture and the teachings of their churches which they felt they were entitled to enjoy.

That our founders were wise is universally accepted. But how did they become so wise? They wanted to do something that had never been done before which was to set up a system of governance that wasn't a theocracy but was based on biblical principles. They wanted a system that would provide order but not trample on the inalienable rights of their constituency. Men would place themselves voluntarily under the authority of the Word of God and use that as a foundation for freely selecting their leaders and governing themselves. Most of the founders were Christian believers and their wisdom came straight from the Word Himself.

They concluded that the new type of government they wanted would include protections against their natural tendencies to usurp God-given freedom. They did the best they could. They based the *Declaration of Independence* and our *Constitution* on biblical principles. But as the decades and centuries go by, the involvement of God in our governance has gradually declined and people are reverting back to their natural tendencies.

But there's good news to be shared. The Bible says that whomever the Son sets free is free indeed (John 6:36). In other words, no matter what happens, the true Christian believer has been set free from sin, death, fear, emotional problems, worry, anxiety, the Adversary, addictions and a host of other things that want to put us in bondage. Indeed, the true believer has been recreated in the image of God and the nature of God is freedom.

Here's the sequence: believe in Jesus → continue in His Word → know the truth → receive your freedom. This will work every single time! But it's the ONLY way to the real FREEDOM of God that our founders used to build a new country.

2 - The Blessing of Freedom

In the previous article, we saw that according to the Bible, ALL Freedom comes from God (2 Corinthians 3:17). Sometimes we take for granted that FREEDOM is one of the great blessings in life that He makes available to those who're willing to receive it, take care of it, defend it, and enjoy it. Among other things, people can use it for making a FREE choice to accept OR reject the Gospel of Jesus Christ. Contrary to popular belief, true biblical Christianity is NOT about pressuring people to accept Jesus, because God as the originator of freedom doesn't work that way.

Have you ever noticed that the freer a country is the more prosperous it seems to become? Another way of saying that is, the freer the country the more closely connected it is to God. We're living in the freest country that's ever existed, and it's also the most PROSPEROUS. By the way, prosperity is a bible word mentioned ninety times there as a BLESSING from God.

Biblical PROSPERITY is closely related to a particular economic system called FREE Enterprise. When FREE Enterprise is grounded in biblical principles, it will ALWAYS be successful and out perform any other economic system ever attempted. But it operates at its best in an environment of universal FREEDOM that can only come from the presence of God. Enterprise without God isn't really free.

PROSPERITY didn't come to us because we were smarter than the rest of the world or because we have more natural resources or because the rest of the world is lazy. No, the driving forces behind American success have been RELIGIOUS FREEDOM and the Christian Bible. We have been FREE to apply ourselves as we want to, believe as we want to and live our lives as we want to BECAUSE we've been willing to involve the Lord of the Bible in our governance. He's the One who makes FREEDOM available to people. In fact, when left to ourselves, we-the-people will ALWAYS work toward restricting freedom so we can control others. God has to stay involved or people on their own will eventually ruin everything.

Until recently, average family income in the US had been declining for decades. Employment had also been decreasing. Is it possible that these things were the predictable result of efforts by many Americans to reduce the involvement of God in our culture? According to the Bible, He doesn't want His involvement reduced but He allows it to happen if that's what people want. All we have to do is reduce religious freedom by restricting God's involvement in our way of life. Of course, when we do that, the purity of the FREE Enterprise system becomes corrupted which causes PROSPERITY and blessing to decline.

The bottom line is if we want our country to preserve its historical PROSPERITY, there's a strong argument to be made for defending FREEDOM. Even for those who don't like bible-based Christianity, the facts of history are irrefutable: FREEDOM prospers. Even for the many who would choose to use their freedom to reject Jesus, they would be way better off economically to support bible-based governance anyway because it's the ONLY road that ever leads to real economic blessing.

3 - The Stewardship of Freedom

As you now know from previous articles, the Bible says freedom was God's idea and that Jesus came so all people could be free. To reiterate it clearly says that knowing the TRUTH is what sets us free (John 8:32), that Jesus is the TRUTH (John 14:6) and that wherever His SPIRIT is present, there's FREEDOM (2 Corinthians 3:17).

The folks who started our country must surely have been some of the wisest people who ever walked the planet. Many of them had grown up during the *First Great Awakening* (1730-1755) and had learned from their Pastors that true freedom comes ONLY from God. At the same time, they were living under an English monarchy that was progressively suppressing their freedom. So, they concluded that the new type of government they wanted would be based on biblical principles and would include protections against the natural tendencies of governments and people to usurp God-given freedom.

Today we see many of our freedoms being threatened just as those wise forefathers predicted would happen if we ever took God out of governance. Part of our problem is that we've failed to fully acknowledge that all real freedom DOES come from Him. And like all His gifts, it was given with a responsibility on our part to protect it from any influences that would try to destroy it. The truth is, we protect what we value; and if we aren't protecting our freedom today, isn't that most likely the result of NOT valuing this precious gift as we should?

How we use God's gifts is called STEWARDSHIP. A steward is someone appointed to manage and be responsible for something that belongs to another person. The Bible says everything belongs to God which makes all of us stewards over His belongings. Freedom is one of those belongings. He's made it available to us and as good stewards we should value it because of where it came from.

We're instructed to take care of it so it can produce its assigned purpose. Everything God says and does has a related purpose. The PURPOSE of God's freedom is to create an environment where the Gospel can be FREELY communicated so that everyone will have a fair chance to FREELY accept or reject Christ.

Someday Christian believers will be asked to account for our assignments. How did we handle the FREEDOM God gave us in this special country of ours? Did we value it and give it a high priority? Did we pray for it and for the leaders called to implement it? Did we vote responsibly to celebrate the authority God has given us to participate in the selection of our own leaders? Did we defend our FREEDOM in the face of those who would do it harm? Did we use it wisely so that those coming behind us will be assured of being able to hear the Gospel?

To God, Freedom is a really big deal. And so is being a good steward. What will we be able to say when Jesus asks us some day what we did with His FREEDOM? Were we good and faithful stewards of it or were we unrighteous stewards (Luke 16:1-13)?

4 - The Pursuit of Freedom

This is the fourth in a series of articles about FREEDOM in America. In previous articles we discussed that according to the Bible, ALL Freedom comes from God. In fact, its very existence requires His presence (2 Corinthians 3:17). Further, we concluded that God's BEST for people is that we live in FREEDOM so that people are able to freely accept OR reject the Gospel of Jesus Christ.

Whatever God makes available is something everyone should eagerly PURSUE because EVERYTHING He gives is GOOD. Certainly, FREEDOM is one of those GOOD things that ALL people desire. And historically, the ones who've experienced it the most are the ones who've encouraged God's involvement. When God is directing things, FREEDOM will always be one of the attending benefits. Along the way, people will have to resist the temptation to restrict His involvement which He WILL allow us to do if that's our choice even though the consequence will ALWAYS be the loss of FREEDOM.

Surely in the history of the world, the special people who led the founding of America understood this relationship better than anybody ever has. One of the main things that defined them was that many were coming out of one of the great Christian revivals in history called the *First Great Awakening* that occurred between about 1730 and 1755. Millions were saved and a revamped Christianity emerged that focused more on the divine destiny of individuals.

One of the facts in our history is that during the second half of the 18th century the American clergy took a leading role in RESISTING the unrighteous authority of the English Monarchy. They understood the biblical principle that FREEDOM could only come to a country by way of a healthy relationship with God on a national level and they boldly taught this idea to their congregations. The British themselves said after the Revolutionary War that had it not been for the influence of the *"Black Robed Regiment*," they would not have lost. The historical truth is, many pastors and ministers fought the enemy in the field LEADING the members of their congregations into battle. They considered that the PURSUIT of individual freedom was worth it, a gift of great value from God that required His involvement and their direct, hands-on leadership.

That's why biblical principles are at the core of our founding documents for all to see. It's also why the various personal writings both public and private of our Founding Fathers warned against ever trying to remove God from government. Did you know that President George Washington dedicated America to God on April 30, 1789 during his inauguration speech in New York City? Historians say that only two countries in history have been so dedicated by their principal government leaders: the United States and Israel.

In sum, FREEDOM and the presence of God ALWAYS go together. They are inseparable. Even though some folks may try to revise history, the truth is what it is: there were those in 1776 who knew the value of freedom, knew that it came from Christ and were willing to PURSUE it at the risk of losing personal possessions and life itself. Against all odds, they were willing to PURSUE God's best for their new country and RESIST the greatest military presence in the world. And they won!

5 - The Value of Freedom

Today (Memorial Day) is a good day to be thankful for our FREEDOM. That's because true God-given FREEDOM has great value, something to be honored and esteemed even if many of us take it for granted. Surely though, we can be thankful today that for more than two hundred years, Americans have been the freest people who ever lived.

The most important thing about true and lasting FREEDOM is that it's always accompanied by the presence of God (2 Corinthians 3:17). That's what makes it so desirable. On the other hand, people are incapable of originating true FREEDOM. We can only restrict and diminish it. Our natural human tendency is to dominate other humans to bring them into servitude and bondage. That's why the six-thousand-year history of the planet has so few examples of FREEDOM among its nations.

Occasionally people have tried to institute freedom without God, but it didn't last. Human-designed freedom is too fragile, an imitation incapable of enduring. But whatever God makes has within its nature the forces of perfection and eternity. God doesn't make temporary things. However, they only endure as long as He continues to be present with them.

Once established though, true FREEDOM will never be abandoned by God. It will ALWAYS be people separating it from His presence that cause its failure. People who love God know better than to try to take over the operation of His special gifts. They're too valuable to tamper with. But unfortunately, most people don't know God.

In fact, many people think they can increase the value of God-made FREEDOM by adding manmade values to it. God's FREEDOM isn't fair enough, it's not equitable or tolerant enough, it's not correct enough and it's too religious. In fact, the presence of God makes some people feel uncomfortable so let's denigrate those who talk about Him so everyone can feel more comfortable with some better freedom than the one God gives.

But, the FREEDOM of God is something of unmatchable value. People down through the ages have longed for it, but in the end when it was offered, they didn't want the One who comes with it. His presence is what makes it so valuable. True FREEDOM and the Presence of God are inseparable and that's the essence of it.

Christians should know this. We should know that true FREEDOM is a special gift from God to be honored and held in high esteem. That's why it's hard to understand how almost 50% of professing American Christians aren't registered to vote. It's hard to understand how only half of registered

Christians actually do vote. And it's hard to understand how half of the ones who do vote align themselves with unbiblical agendas that work against God's FREEDOM. The fact is, it's our responsibility to preserve God's FREEDOM to protect the ones who don't know any better for as long as we can.

When something is perceived to have great value, the proper response is genuine gratitude. We can show our appreciation by honoring and esteeming it and by thanking the One who loved us enough to make it available. We can also stop tampering with it acknowledging that it isn't possible to improve it.

Indeed friend, there's no such thing as secular FREEDOM. It will never work and it won't endure. But the FREEDOM God gives has great value that will last forever. That's why today's a good day to be grateful.

6 - The Defense of Freedom

This is the final article in a series about FREEDOM in America. Previously we saw that according to the Bible, ALL Freedom comes from God and its very existence requires His presence (2 Corinthians 3:17). So, we concluded that God's intention for all people is that we live in FREEDOM. The truth of history is that the people and the nations that've been the FREEST are the ones that were able to develop and hold onto a close relationship with God.

FREEDOM is a condition that all people naturally desire, so much so that sometimes we're willing to put at risk the things that are most important to us in order to obtain and hold onto it. During the Revolutionary War, there were more than 50,000 American casualties from 1776 to 1783 as our forefathers fought against the world's mightiest military force in pursuit of an opportunity to try a system of governance based on the principles of Bible-based FREEDOM. The odds were against them. Tens of thousands of colonists faced imprisonment and the loss of their estates or execution as traitors if England had prevailed. But for them, just the possibility of such FREEDOM was worth the risk.

Once real FREEDOM has been obtained though, it has to be DEFENDED or it will deteriorate and eventually be lost. There are always people who want to control other people because that's our nature. Many of those same folks don't like God very much and resent FREEDOM because it's God-given. Out of this comes the same question America faced in 1776: is FREEDOM important enough to risk everything?

If our answer is yes, then it's vital to understand what has to be done in DEFENSE of something so desirable yet so fragile:

1. Because we have FREEDOM, God allows us to participate in the process of establishing our own leadership. So, we have the vital responsibility of voting. Yet half of professing Christians in America aren't even registered to vote. And on average half of registered Christians don't turn out to vote.

2. Not only should Christians vote, but we should also do whatever's necessary to be INFORMED voters. Then we should vote according to what's best for the Kingdom of God, <u>not our personal agendas or the agendas of our political affiliations</u>, but the Kingdom's agenda.

3. What's best for the Kingdom of God is what the Bible says is best. So, to be a defender of freedom, we need to study our Bibles so we know what God's priorities are. Sometimes Christians vote with values in mind that haven't come from a righteous source and if we don't vote with God in mind then the consequence will eventually be loss of freedom.

4. Finally, a successful DEFENSE requires that we stand for Truth as defined by God. When people try to take away our freedom, we have to RESIST the loss of such a valuable possession. If we don't RESIST, if we don't take a stand for Truth, if we won't DEFEND our FREEDOM even in the face of suffering personal loss, we'll gradually lose this wonderful, special gift from God.

Jesus said to seek first the Kingdom of God in all things. Thus, what's best for the Kingdom should be what guides us in all things. We'll either do our part with God's help to DEFEND our FREEDOM or gradually lose a precious gift God intends for us to possess and enjoy forever.

THE AUTHOR

ABOUT THE AUTHOR

Dr. Bill Miller is an ordained cross-denominational minister, elder and the founder of a national nonprofit Christian organization called *Make A Way Ministries.*

He has been involved in family counseling and teaching since 1985 and has assisted tens of thousands of families in the area of overcoming financial problems.

He also pastored the bilingual (English/Spanish) *Faith Life Fellowship Church* in Miami Florida.

Dr. Miller has published a bible-based financial e-newsletter called *Prosperous Life Newsletter* since January 1998 and has written more than 40 books and e-books about various financial, administrative and ministry topics.

This is his first endeavor in what will undoubtedly be called a political publication even though it's actually dealing with the Kingdom of God.

Feel free to write to Dr. Miller with comments or to arrange a book-signing:

P.O. Box 1164
Granbury, Texas 76048

A WORD ABOUT MAKE A WAY MINISTRIES

Make A Way Ministries is a nationally recognized nonprofit (501c3) Christian and bible-based counseling ministry. The Ministry has operated continuously since September 1987 assisting tens of thousands of families across the nation to overcome credit and financial problems.

The mission of MAWM is to lead people out of debt and to educate families so they can be victorious in overcoming financial difficulties. This publication is part of that ministry.

If you would like to consider a donation to Make A Way Ministries it would be seed sown into good ground and would make it possible for the ministry to help more families. Please send your donations to:

Make A Way Ministries
PO Box 1164
Granbury, Texas 76048

If you have any questions about the ministry, please feel free to call us Monday through Friday from 9:00 AM to 5:30 PM Central time: (800) 357-4223.

Also, you are welcome to subscribe to our weekly bible-based e-newsletter called Prosperous Life Newsletter published continuously since January 1998 by going to the following link:

http://www.creditcounseling.net/prosperous-life-newsletter.aspx

ENDNOTES

Introduction
[1] Deuteronomy 30:19

Chapter One
[2] John 1:14
[3] John 17:13-21
[4] John 3:19-21
[5] 2 Corinthians 4:4
[6] *Merriam-Webster.com Dictionary*, Merriam-Webster, https://www.merriam-webster.com/dictionary/politically%20correct. Accessed 12 Apr. 2021.
[7] Daniel 12:8-9, 1 Peter 1:10-11, 2 Peter 1:20-21, 1 Corinthians 2:9-13, 1 Thessalonians 2:13, 2 Timothy 3:16 https://www.blueletterbible.org/faq/don_stewart/don_stewart_420.cfm
[8] John 14:6, Proverbs 30:5
[9] Numbers 23:19, Hebrews 13:8, James 1:17
[10] 1 Corinthians 2:9-13
[11] 2 Timothy 3:16
[12] James 1:14
[13] Matthew 28:18-20
[14] Hebrews 13:8 and Malachi 3:6

Chapter Two
[15] 1 John 4:8, 16
[16] Mark 12:31
[17] Matthew 23:16
[18] Matthew 23:17
[19] Matthew 23:27
[20] Matthew 23:33
[21] Ibid
[22] Luke 11:44
[23] Ibid
[24] Matthew 21: 12-13, Mark 11:15-18 and John 2:13-17
[25] Genesis 6:9 through 9:17

Chapter Three

[26] Acts 17:26-27

[27] Genesis 9:1, 7

[28] Genesis 9:7

[29] Deuteronomy 32:9

[30] Exodus 18:25

[31] Matthew 28:18

[32] https://bible.knowing-jesus.com/topics/Borders

[33] Numbers 20:14-21

[34] Deuteronomy 24:14-15

[35] Exodus 12:13

[36] Leviticus 16:29-30

[37] Leviticus 17:8-12

Chapter Four

[38] Zechariah 7:8-10

[39] Jeremiah 22:3-5

[40] Exodus 12:49

[41] Deuteronomy 1:16

[42] Hebrews 13:2

[43] Matthew 28:19

[44] Acts 1:8

[45] Matthew 12:34, 23:33

[46] Romans 10:14

[47] Matthew 4:1-11

Chapter Five

[48]https://www.google.com/search?q=Define%3A+refugee&ie=utf-8&oe=utf-8&client=firefox-b-1

[49]https://en.m.wikipedia.org/wiki/Asylum_in_the_United_States

[50] Galatians 3:25, Romans 3:6-9, 6:14, 7:4-6, 10:4

[51] Hebrews 11:6

Chapter Six

[52] https://www.boundless.com/immigration-resources/u-s-citizenship-requirements/#military-and-civil-service-registration

[53] Proverbs 4:7

[54] Ephesians 1:17-18
[55] Proverbs 1:7
[56] 2 Corinthians 3:17

Chapter Seven
[57] Hosea 4:6
[58] https://openborders.info/open-borders-manifesto/
[59]http://encyclopedia.densho.org/Naturalization_Act_of_1790/
[60]http://encyclopedia.densho.org/Naturalization_Act_of_1790/
[61]https://en.wikipedia.org/wiki/List_of_United_States_immigration_laws
[62] Ibid
[63] Statue of Liberty-Ellis Island Foundation, www.ellisisland.org https://www.uscis.gov/history-and-genealogy/our-history/agency-history/early-american-immigration-policies
[64] Ibid

Chapter Eight
[65] https://openborders.info/open-borders-manifesto/
[66] 1 Corinthians 6:9-10
[67] Matthew 25:15
[68] Galatians 6:7

Chapter Nine
[69] Ibid

Chapter Ten
[70]https://en.wikipedia.org/wiki/Mexico%E2%80%93United_States_border
[71] https://en.wikipedia.org/wiki/Secure_Fence_Act_of_2006
[72] https://en.wikipedia.org/wiki/Secure_Fence_Act_of_2006
[73] https://www.politifact.com/truth-o-meter/statements/2017/apr/23/mick-mulvaney/fact-check-did-top-democrats-vote-border-wall-2006/
[74]https://gop.com/democrats-then-vs-now-on-border-wall-funding/
[75] Matthew 24:12
[76]https://www.americanimmigrationcouncil.org/research/how-united-states-immigration-system-works

[77] https://www.merriam-webster.com/dictionary/alien
[78] Revelation 21:12
[79] Revelation 21:8

Chapter Eleven
[80] https://americanvision.org/1644/choose-day-whose-notes-will-follow/
[81] Psalm 22:27-28
[82]https://www.archives.gov/exhibits/american_originals/inaugtxt.html
[83] From William J. Johnson, *George Washington, The Christian* (New York: The Abingdon Press, 1919). See also: http://www.cbn.com/spirituallife/prayerandcounseling/intercession/washington_prayer.aspx?mobile=false
[84] Matthew 16:18

Chapter Twelve
[85] John 17:13-21
[86] 1 John 3:20
[87] 2 Corinthians 5:20
[88] Matthew 22:39
[89] Matthew 5:44
[90] James 3:17
[91] 2 Corinthians 4:4
[92] Isaiah 10:27
[93] http://reclaimamericaforchrist.org/2010/12/20/the-black-robed-regiment-preachers-who-fought/
[94] John 2:13, Matthew 21:12-13, Mark 11:15-16, Luke 19:45
[95] Matthew 19:26
[96] Romans 14:4 and 30:10
[97] Romans 13:1

Appendix A
[98]https://www.archives.gov/exhibits/american_originals/inaugtxt.html

www.ingramcontent.com/pod-product-compliance
Lightning Source LLC
LaVergne TN
LVHW051633080426
835511LV00016B/2321